GIOVANNI'S RING

GIOVANNI'S RING

MY LIFE INSIDE
THE *REAL*
SOPRANOS

GIOVANNI ROCCO
WITH DOUGLAS SCHOFIELD

CHICAGO
REVIEW
PRESS

Justice is a temporary thing that must at last come to an end; but the conscience is eternal and will never die.

—Martin Luther, 1530

CONTENTS

NOTE TO READERS

SOME NAMES OF INDIVIDUALS and identifying details mentioned in this book have been fictionalized. Any similarity between the fictionalized names and the names of real people is strictly coincidental. For the author's own protection, the name Giovanni Rocco is also a pseudonym, but the undercover identity Giovanni Gatto is the real one he used to infiltrate the New Jersey Mafia.

1

A DAY IN THE LIFE

IT WAS FIVE on a rainy afternoon in November when Luigi called me. The newly made member of the DeCavalcante crime family wanted a meeting.

His voice dripped with self-importance: "I need a couple of cases. I'm at the club. Come over." A meeting on his turf for only two cases of contraband cigarettes? It made no sense. I knew he had another motive.

"I'm busy," I said dismissively. "I'm over in Union right now. Call you later."

By now, I was acutely aware of widening divisions in the family, not only over who should replace John Riggi, the aging DeCavalcante boss, but also over Luigi Oliveri's swaggering behavior since the old man had given him his button at a secret ceremony. Riggi had conducted that ceremony without consulting the rest of the family, the Gambino bosses, or any other *borgata*.

Based on my interactions with Oliveri up to this point, I had a bad, bad feeling about his call. Every instinct was telling me the cigarette deal was just a ruse to set me up—to injure me or, more likely, to whack me out. "Lui the Dog," as he was known (or often, mockingly, "the Pet" or "the Mutt"), was itching to send a message to my capo, Charlie Stango, and to others in the Administration, that he was ready and able to use violence, inside or outside the organization, to make a point.

When the Dog called, I was standing in Marco Barone's auto body shop. Marco was a longtime Gambino associate, and the guy sure as hell looked and sounded the part: overweight, double chin, rasping voice, and a perpetual cigar stub in his mouth. (We sometimes called him "Sammy Cigars.") I'd been doing a lot of business with Marco in the last few months, selling him cigarettes and assorted swag, but today I was hoping he could help me track down an aluminum welder to repair one of the dump trucks at the excavation company where I kept my office. Charlie Stango's son Whitey had been driving the truck, and he'd damaged the load bed.

Luigi called two more times. Each time I told him I was still busy and didn't have time to drive over to his club to deliver the cigarettes. I could tell from his tone that my response offended him, and I knew why. In his eyes, he was the only made member in this conversation, and therefore the only one who counted. I was, as he'd once derided me to my face, "just a fuckin' citizen."

He kept insisting that I come to him because it was raining and the traffic was heavy. He claimed it would take forever for him to come to me. This was bullshit and I knew it. His social club was no more than a fifteen-minute ride away. I said, "Take your time. I'll wait for you."

The perceived arrogance of my reply pissed him off even more. He growled that he'd have to find a ride and it would just be better that I come to him.

My gut was telling me I'd be walking into a trap—and I always listened to my gut. And there were other considerations. To maintain my credibility within the family, it was time to put this fucker in his place. As Charlie had told me, "You gotta go at this guy head on, Giovanni! Be the man you were born to be!" If I didn't, I would lose face in the family, and I would lose the trust of my crew. Worse, it would mean losing Charlie's trust. That alone could cost me my life.

At that moment, I was completely on my own. I had a cover team backing me, but from past experience I knew I couldn't count on a quick response if things went south. And I couldn't call in my own street crew, because that might lead to a bloodbath.

I was in a tight spot. There was no way I could risk going into Luigi's neighborhood, but there were too many risks to our overall operation, too many moving parts, for me to just walk away and go home for the night.

I made a battlefield decision and told Marco Barone about my ongoing problems with Lui the Dog. After laying out the background, I put it to him squarely. "I think the bastard's trying to set me up."

Marco's reaction was typically direct: "Fuck this guy, Giovanni! If you don't trust him, make him come here! I ain't leavin' for a while. I can wait with ya, and I've got some guys coming over to hang out and have coffee. We're gonna settle up some things. Tell him if he wants those cigarettes, he's gonna have to come here."

Earlier, I had been thinking it would be a bad idea for me to invite Luigi to another family's hangout. I had a few Gambino friends, but I had no status in their family, so how was that going to look? But when Marco gave me the green light, my protocol worries evaporated. I thought, *This could work.* If the body shop was loaded up with some serious guys and Luigi saw that I had a solid relationship with the Gambinos, and not just few DeCav stepchildren, that might put him in his place. It would definitely make him think twice about taking a shot at me.

True to form, Luigi called again, raging about the rain and the traffic and how I absolutely must come to him. I stuck to my position. "If you want those cigarettes, you'll just have to come here." Past experience had taught me how easy it was to bait him, so I softened my tone slightly and added, "Look, Lui, no shit. I really am tied up here. I've gotta find an aluminum welder for one of our dump trucks. Any chance you know anyone?"

He went for it. "You got dump trucks? What kind of company you into?"

"An excavation company, and I really need to get this truck back on the road."

Immediately, his whole manner changed and he was full of questions. It was obvious he wanted to see what kind of racket I had going on so close to his neighborhood.

"Where are you? I'll come over."

I gave him the body shop's name and address.

"I'll be there soon."

Minutes after that call, the rear area of the body shop started filling up with Gambino guys. One of the first to arrive was Danny "Gooms"

Bertelli, and that was perfect for me. Bertelli was one of my capo's oldest and closest friends. With him there, at least I began to feel comfortable, telling myself I was in a good place. I thought, *God help Luigi if he says something stupid.*

And then it all went to shit.

I overheard Gooms telling Marco that he'd been talking to Nick ("Nicky the Whip" Milano—a Philly mob soldier) and he was on his way over. He said Nick had mentioned some other guys who'd be coming by as well, and he rattled off some names. Then he said, "Oh, yeah . . . Nicky says Kyle's coming. Ragusa. Be here soon."

Kyle Ragusa? When I heard that name, I could barely breathe. Kyle Ragusa was a Gambino thug I had arrested in 2007.

Back then, I'd been part of a federal task force involved in a racketeering investigation called Operation Family Ties. We arrested a couple of dozen Gambino family members, including Ragusa. Because of that investigation, I knew Ragusa to be a thug who gloried in violence. He was the quintessential Mafia enforcer, unwavering in his determination to maintain his place within the family and always ready to do anything his bosses ordered. His record of convictions included multiple assaults and a stabbing, but his main claim to fame—and all-important respect— was taking the rap for a crime he *didn't* commit. He had served a multi- year prison sentence for a shooting that had actually been carried out by his Gambino skipper, Andy Merola.

I knew I could be in deep trouble if Ragusa showed up, but I couldn't let that show. While I continued talking and laughing with Marco and Gooms and the other guys as they arrived, my mind was racing, trying to calculate how I could avoid ending up in a landfill.

The voice of reason in my head was telling me to get out of there: *Forget the fact that Luigi Oliveri is on his way over, you idiot! Leave now!* But a disappearing act was going to look really strange, especially to Marco Barone and Gooms Bertelli, after I'd made such an issue to both of them about this guy I was supposedly waiting for.

There was no way out. Cold, hard reality was telling me I was a dead man walking, so I started mentally prepping myself. I wouldn't go down without a fight.

Nicky the Whip and Kyle Ragusa arrived together. When they came busting in through the side door, Ragusa was just as I remembered him—tall, hard-muscled, shaved head. The second he arrived, he started yukking it up, yelling and guffawing, doing the whole wiseguy routine, trying to be the center of attention: "Hey, hey, hey!" "How ya doin'?" "Hey, look at dis fuckin' guy!" I had watched those same antics on many nights of surveillance when I was tailing him, taking photos and videos of his movements. On one night in particular, I had actually held the door for him, his skipper Merola, and Nicky Scarfo Jr. as we all exited the Palm Restaurant at the Tropicana Casino in Atlantic City.

Watching Ragusa now, I thought, *How is this guy not going to recognize me?*

He was in the room now, and there was nothing I could do but ride it out. The only thing I had going for me was the passage of time since the 2007 arrest, and that seemed like a pretty faint hope.

Marco Barone started walking him around, introducing him to guys in the room he didn't know. As I watched, I could see Ragusa assessing the company. He must have realized he was nowhere near being highest rung on the ladder, because his behavior visibly changed.

The mob has a simple dress code. The men who dress properly and look polished are the top guys, the ones who give the orders and the ones to be feared. Ordinary soldiers, especially the muscle, dress down—T-shirts, sweatshirts, jeans, boots. They are the low guys in the hierarchy, the ones who take the orders and do the dirty work. They have no need for nice clothes.

Like a good guard dog, Ragusa looked around, took in how everyone was dressed, and came to heel. Eventually, Marco led him over to me. "Kyle, this is Giovanni. He's with Charlie Stango. Remember Charlie?" In that fateful, heart-stopping second, as our eyes locked, I was sure my cover was about to be blown.

Ragusa greeted me with a blank look and said, "Oh yeah. Nice to meet ya, Giovanni."

By some miracle that I will never understand, there wasn't even a hint of recognition. For some reason, maybe due to the environment and the setting—a mob gathering where no one would expect to meet some cop who had arrested him many years ago—Ragusa just greeted me with total respect and moved on.

I kept on talking to whoever I'd been talking to, praying that the guy wouldn't take a second look and come back at me with the terrifying musings of a mob enforcer who's searching his memory: *Giovanni, you know, you look familiar. Haven't we met? Wait a minute! You look like . . .*

My guts were still churning twenty minutes later when my cell phone rang. It was Luigi. He was outside the shop. I told him to wait and I'd be right out with the cigarettes.

The moment I walked outside, the Dog stepped out of the front passenger seat of a Ford SUV. One of his gorillas was sitting behind the wheel, and another one was in the rear. I didn't recognize either of them.

He stood in place next to the vehicle, waiting for me to deliver the two cases, waiting with his predictable arrogance for me to come to him. After the transaction was done, his gaze shifted to the unimposing brick front of the building behind me. He started right in with the questions— "So what's this place? Whose place is this? Is this your place?"—all the while trying to peer past me.

"It's not mine. It's this guy Danny's place. He's a friend of mine. His friend Marco lets me use it when I'm in the area."

The expression on his face changed. "Danny?" he asked. "'Soft Shoes' guy? I think I know him. I think I might have been here."

I doubted he knew Gooms, but he had just handed me a perfect opportunity to stick it to him. "Oh, you know him? He's inside. Come on in and say hello."

Without giving him a chance to answer, I walked him into the front of the shop. Most of the lights were off, but I couldn't miss the hungry look on the maggot's face as he took in the high-end office furniture and the chrome wheel-rim displays mounted on the walls. This was the space where Marco Barone met with his customers and where he and I usually met when we were counting out cash from our deals.

The back office area was lit up, and the strong smell of Marco's cigar smoke was drifting through the building. We could hear everyone shouting and laughing over their espressos. I couldn't have staged the scene better if I'd been a Hollywood director.

"Whaddya got? A party going on in here?" Tough guy Luigi sounded a bit nervous, and I liked that.

"Nah, just some of my guys," I answered, level and cool. I yelled to the back, "Hey Gooms! Out here! Somebody says he knows you! Wants to say hello!"

Danny Bertelli strolled out to the front, curious to see who claimed to know him. He was dressed in his usual designer duds, looking every inch the polished and intimidating Gambino heavyweight I had come to know. His face wore a disdainful expression that said, *Who's talking about me without my permission?*

Luigi quickly realized that this guy wasn't the Danny he knew. He tried to shrug it off, but Bertelli wasn't having that. He demanded to know exactly who Luigi thought he was. After listening to Luigi's stammering explanation, Bertelli explained in his inimitable, lethal way that he would never be confused for Soft Shoes because that kid was a *chooch*.

"So . . . who are you?" Bertelli's tone made it sound like he was talking to an insect.

A bit too proudly, Luigi explained his status within the DeCavalcante family. Gooms responded by explaining his own status in just three words: "I'm with Nino." That's Nino Molinelli, the John Gotti guy. In other words, *I'm a Gambino, peasant boy. Who the fuck are you?*

The Dog was way, way out of his league, and he knew it. He must have figured the only way to save face was to talk bad about me—*me*, a close associate of Charlie Stango. Charlie was a highly respected capo in his own DeCavalcante crime family and, crucially, a longtime friend of Gooms Bertelli.

Luigi pointed at me and asked Bertelli, "How do you know this clown?"

My blood went cold. I moved closer. "What did you just say?"

Luigi doubled down, bragging to Gooms, with me standing right there, how he'd wanted me to come to his social club tonight. Once I got there, he said, his guys were ready to drag me down to the basement to answer some questions that needed asking. He said if that didn't go well, I wouldn't have been leaving.

There it was. I had listened to my gut, and my gut had been right. The bastard had been planning to whack me out. "You motherfucker!" I snarled.

This was a critical moment. I had Danny Bertelli watching me, and after what Luigi had just said, a real mob guy would have grabbed Luigi by the throat. If I had done that, Gooms could have taken it as a green light to call out the boys from the back. Luigi might have ended up severely injured or even dead. In my position, I did not want to be responsible for that. So now I was walking a tightrope—acting like I was ready for blood, but holding back.

Unwittingly, Gooms came to the rescue. "Giovanni, how do you know this guy? This guy's a piece of work." Before I could answer, he turned back to Luigi. "You *do* know he's with Charlie Stango?" His voice dripped with the dark threat of violence as he added, "I've known Giovanni for a while. He's a good guy, and"—pronouncing the words slowly—"*he's a friend of mine.*"

Luigi visibly shrank. He immediately tried to deflect, jabbering about how, oh yeah, he knows Charlie, and how he and Charlie had a long history together from the neighborhood. Then, pathetically, he tried to tell a war story about Charlie from when Luigi was a kid.

Bertelli abruptly cut him off. He gave him a little free advice, saying that he shouldn't talk too freely about "my dear friend Charlie" and that "Giovanni also has a lot of friends." The message couldn't have been clearer. Luigi said a quick, respectful good-bye and asked me to walk out with him.

Outside, the conversation became suddenly civil. The Dog's tail was firmly tucked between his legs. He had just come within an inch of a getting his ass kicked, or worse, and he knew it. Now that I had completely turned the tables on him, he lamely tried to save face by telling me that Gooms was a good guy and knows a lot of people—talking as if he knew all about Danny Bertelli and I knew nothing.

I laid it on with my response: "Yeah. He's a great guy, and a very respected guy."

He quickly changed the subject. "You should have told me you had an excavation company. I could help you get contracts."

He was almost begging me to dial it down, so I said, "Yeah. Look, Lui, I got no beefs with you. I only want to do business."

He quickly agreed and said we should talk again. We parted ways, and I walked back into the shop with a feeling that I might have just dodged a bullet—twice, with Luigi and with Ragusa. But I wasn't prepared for what came next.

While I was outside, Gooms had been on the phone, calling Nevada, telling my boss Charlie Stango all about his conversation with Luigi, and what a jerkoff the kid was, and how he'd wanted to punch him in the face.

Within what felt like seconds, Charlie called me on my cellphone. As soon as I answered, he started yelling at me. "What the fuck is going on out there, Giovanni? Why the fuck are you bringing that scumbag to that place? If you two can't get along, then just go the other fucking way! Are you crazy, bringing him to that house? Now he knows what you're doing and where you are! You two are gonna start World War III! He's gonna say or do something stupid, and I'm gonna have to get on a plane and come out there and take care of it! You can't bring him to another *borgata*! That's the Gambinos' house. Now he knows, and if they do something to him because he does something stupid, you're gonna start a fucking war!"

From the frying pan to the fire. I'd got things smoothed out with Luigi, but now I was wondering if Charlie might be the one to whack me out if the DeCav Administration found out what had just happened.

It was a huge comfort to return to my real life late that night—or so I thought. My troubles weren't quite over.

My wife was totally pissed off. I had promised her I'd be home a lot earlier. "Dinner's done!" she snapped at me. "The dishes are done! Everything's done! I could have used some help with the kids, but now they're in bed! Why did you even bother to come home?"

I tried to explain what happened, to put her at ease, but she didn't want to hear about it. She stormed off to the bedroom.

2

THE UNIVERSITY
OF BAYONNE

I WAS BORN AND RAISED IN BAYONNE, New Jersey. Bergen Point was my neighborhood, so I was a "downtown boy." Bayonne isn't very big—less than six square miles of land—but like a lot of places, it was socially divided. In local parlance, if you lived south of the old Eighth Street train station, you were a "downtowner."

There were no malls in those days. You shopped on Broadway, which was one of Bayonne's main north-south arteries. That street was booming—just like the one in New York City, as we liked to tell ourselves—and very seldom did we feel the need to leave Bayonne for shopping or services. When I was issued a school uniform, my mom would send me three doors down to an old Italian lady. She didn't speak any English, but that didn't matter. She'd take me into her house, stand me up on a wooden box, hem my pants, and send me home. Another Old World aspect I remember was a fruit truck that would come by regularly, driven by an Italian guy selling apples and peaches. It was a great neighborhood, and it was a good mix.

Overall, the best way to describe Bayonne would be "self-contained." No matter what their respective lifestyle and backgrounds, the residents tended to rely on one other. Whether you were a cop, a mob guy, a laborer, a truck driver, or a merchant didn't matter. In a strange way, despite the city's internal divisions, people watched out for one another.

I went to a Catholic school, did poorly, and got in a lot of trouble. My father, a Vietnam vet, was an honest and well-respected cop in Hudson County, but that didn't discourage me from spending too much time hanging around with the wrong element. Even as a kid, I got to know and interact with Mafia guys, usually through playmates whose families were connected. Back then, MOTBY, the Military Ocean Terminal at Bayonne, was in full operation on the city's eastern shore, and much of the local economy was focused on that facility. Although it was a military base, it created a lot of waterfront jobs for locals—and a lot of those jobs were controlled by New York's Genovese crime family. John DiGilio Sr. was the local boss in those days.

Unsurprisingly, the blue-collar environment in Bayonne produced some pretty tough people. For example, Chuck Wepner was raised in Bayonne. He was the boxer whose 1975 heavyweight title fight with Muhammad Ali inspired Sylvester Stallone to write the script for *Rocky*. Wepner famously said of Bayonne, "This was a tough town with a lot of people from the docks and the naval base, and you had to fight to survive." That might have been a bit of an exaggeration, but the city's employment demographics were indeed pretty well defined: street thug, longshoreman, mobster, cop, retail clerk, or businessman—there weren't a lot of in-betweens. There were racial and ethnic tensions, too, but people from other neighborhoods knew to stay out of your neighborhood, and you knew to stay out of theirs. You didn't step over the line, because you knew you'd get your ass beaten. I'm not proud to admit that I was part of that, but in those days few people dared speak out against it. That was just the way it was. And yet somehow, at least in my experience, everyone seemed to mesh and respect one another.

Of course, it wasn't all peace and love. My family lived right next to a tavern. There was a stoop out front, and on hot summer nights, the whole family would sit out there. As a kid, it was nothing for me to see a bar fight spill out onto the street, see the police arrive to break it up, or see my dad step in when he didn't like the odds and beat the hell out of somebody.

As you might guess, my poor attitude at school and my choice of company became sources of deep disappointment for my honest cop father. Both of my parents had been raised in the projects. They had married in their late teens and started out with nothing. Most of their young lives were spent in an ongoing struggle to provide for their three children in the best way they possibly could. I grew up knowing that my dad's grandfather had been beaten to death in the street, and that his father had abandoned his wife and kids and died early. With that personal background, my father had been forced to grow up fast and strong, and he expected me and my brother to exhibit the same maturity and strength.

I knew from personal experience, as an awed witness, that my dad never backed down from a fight, and his fear-no-man approach to life was exactly how he raised us. Consequently, there were times when he dealt with us in the same way as he dealt with some of the thugs and drunks he arrested: hands on. Predictably, as I got older, battles ensued when I tried to turn the tables by applying his never-back-down attitude to my own conflicts with him.

Today, my relationship with my father is strong and close. I now understand that it wasn't that he didn't love me; it was just that, having never experienced a true father-son relationship himself, he just wasn't sure *how* to love me. When he worked uniformed patrol, and later as a detective, he wasn't always around in the evenings or on weekends. But he did try, in his own way, to do as much with us as he could. He coached my football team and eventually became the North Jersey president of Pop Warner, the youth football program. But to this day, he looks back and says, "You know, I should've been there more. I really wasn't there to raise you guys. I'm sorry." He carries a lot of guilt over it, and he has openly shared that with me, helping me to understand and grow to love him more as both a father and a trusted friend.

Growing up, I played mostly with Italian and Irish kids in our neighborhood, and some of their family members were associates or made guys in the mob. One connected family lived right around the corner, and their kids were my regular playmates. Their uncle was a crew boss in the Genovese family. The kids knew it and spoke openly about it.

But if that wasn't enough, some family on my mother's side knew members and associates of outlaw biker groups. When I was six years old, one of my aunts married one of these biker guys. The reception was held in my grandmother's apartment in the projects. It was tiny little apartment, and there were all these bodies jammed in there—including a number of bikers decked out in their vests and chains and knives. My mom's father had suffered a stroke, so he was out in the back bedroom. Several kids were there as well, and we were all playing in the living room.

When the time came for the cake-cutting, the crowd converged on the kitchen, spilling out into the front hallway. Previously, the bikers had been passing around a bottle of grappa and hitting it hard. One of them, who was pretty drunk, leaned over the table, scraped a piece of icing off the cake, and flicked it at another guy. He was just screwing around, but soon these brutes were all getting into the act, flicking icing back and forth and destroying the cake.

I still have a vivid memory of what happened next. First, it felt like the whole building was shaking. It wasn't, of course—it was just a sensation caused by the rising tension in the room. It was as if the air itself was vibrating. There were multiple people calling out, "Whoa! Whoa! Wait! Wait!" because they could feel the underlying violence bubbling to the surface. Years later, my father told me that when he realized what was coming, he ducked out of the kitchen and into the hall. Seconds later, the whole place went crazy and a huge fight broke out. One of my aunts grabbed all of us little kids, herded us into the back bathroom, and jammed us into the bathtub. It was one of those big, old cast-iron clawfoot tubs. She pushed us in there in case any shots went off and bullets came through the wall. She was only sixteen at the time, but she'd been around bikers long enough to realize what could happen.

I had friends drawn from the whole economic spectrum of Bayonne life. Some lived in roach-filled apartments, and some, mainly families who were connected to the mob, had the best of everything—granite countertops and in-ground swimming pools. Our family was somewhere in the middle. When I visited my grandmother, the only place to play outside was among the "shit-ems," a common label for the troublemaking dirtbag kids who never aspired to be anything. Other times, I'd be swimming in some mob family's pool.

Although I often hung out with bad guys, to my parents' never-ending frustration, it was probably because of my father that I also knew when to stop. There was a mechanic's shop in town called Harrington's Auto Repair, and sometimes a trusting local who needed work done on his car would leave it parked overnight at the garage with the keys tucked behind a visor. This was common knowledge, so if my delinquent friends decided one night to take one of those cars for a joyride, I might go along, but never as the driver and never in the backseat. I always positioned myself as the front passenger in case the cops stopped us—so I could bail fast. And I always made sure that we left the car where we found it, back at the garage.

Luckily, I never got caught.

Mom and Dad knew the street environment wasn't exactly ideal for us kids, and they tried to do their best for us by getting the family out of the city whenever possible. One day, my mom won a little over $1,000 on the New Jersey Pick 3 lottery, and she used the money to buy a pop-up trailer. From that point on, we got out of the city as much as we could during school holidays, often vacationing in the Catskills.

But, with my dad's personality, things could sometimes get touchy. On one camping trip, my brother cut himself with a saw. He had a huge gash in his leg and obviously needed stitches, but he didn't want my father to know, so he was hiding in the bushes. We had been in the middle of packing up to head home, and my father was yelling, "What are you guys doing? Stop screwing around! Let's go!" When I showed my face in the campsite, he barked, "Where's your brother?"

I didn't want to say, so I went back up the hill, pretending to look for him, and he was still hiding in the brush. He was petrified he'd get in trouble when our father found out he'd slashed his leg open. Dad always had a good heart, but we were never quite sure of how he would deal with certain situations. Thankfully, we got through that incident without too much bellowing.

Thinking back, it's not as if I tried very hard to make things any easier for my mom and dad. I had a bad attitude at school and got left back because of it. (As I always like to say, I enjoyed sixth grade so much, I repeated it.) My brother and sister were both A+ students, but not me. I was the black sheep. When I'd get suspended from school, I'd beat the letter home, remove it from the mail, and make it disappear. Because these were normally three-day suspensions, it was a chance for me to cut out and go to New York City to hang out.

But then one time I got two suspensions back to back—first three days, and then five days—and I failed to beat the second letter home. My dad read the letter and confronted me. "OK, I don't understand how you got suspended for *five* days, right off the bat. How the fuck did that happen?"

I confessed to him that I'd been suspended previously for three days, and now this second suspension was for five days.

"So you got suspended already, and we didn't know about it?"

I came clean: "I took the first letter."

He was furious. He shouted, "You know, the best thing you could do right now is just go kill yourself! Go run in traffic! Get out of my sight!"

My mom jumped in, as she always did when things got too crazy. "Oh, don't talk like that to the boy! Don't say those things to him!" But I was actually relieved. Being told to go kill myself was much better than getting the shit beaten out of me.

As the years passed, I learned to adapt and live with all of Bayonne's different types of people and diverse cultures. Exposure to the violence I have described might sound horrific to some, but it paid off in my adult career, especially in my undercover work, because I was never fazed by anything I saw. When I played at my grandmother's house, I was around outlaw bikers. I knew that life. I knew how those people associated with each other. And then I had the Italian and Irish thing going on in my own neighborhood, so I knew how the adults in those families interacted. I knew how these different types of people spoke, how they lived, what set them off, and what made them happy. From watching my dad and other cops in action, I also learned how good guys and bad guys interacted.

When my father was promoted to detective, he would work major case crimes and come home with photographs of bloody crime scenes, or of floaters, or of body parts washed up in Newark Bay. He sometimes showed these pictures to me, not to torment me but to try to deter me from falling into "that life." The effect of this, over time, was that I became hardened to scenes of violent death. One photograph I'll never forget was an autopsy photo of John DiGilio, the Genovese boss who had controlled the longshoremen's union on the Bayonne waterfront.

Somehow, I navigated through all of this. I don't look back and pity myself for all the turmoil I experienced. Although I never went to college, my childhood and teenage years provided me with a very specialized education—a graduate degree from what I call the "University of Bayonne." The knowledge I gained, and the survival instincts I learned, on the streets of that very fine educational institution were carried into my adult life and remain with me to this day. It was the education I would need for my career as a uniformed cop, as a major crimes detective, and as long-term undercover operative.

It was the education that would keep me alive.

3

ACCIDENTAL COP

BY THE AGE OF SIXTEEN I was failing at school and almost everything else. Bearing in mind that my father's best advice was to kill myself, I decided one day to stop in at an air force recruiting office on my way home from school and try to sign up. This move was driven more by a desire to get away than anything else, but my mother wisely refused to sign the papers.

Over the next two years, I managed to scrape through to my senior year, but I spent most of my time hanging out with crazy people and partying like a rock star. I didn't bother taking the SATs because there was zero chance I was going to college. I had no real direction in life, and I pretty much didn't care. So, by the end of my senior year, it was pretty clear I wasn't going to be allowed to walk the stage for graduation.

As it turned out, my history teacher rescued me from that humiliation, but not for altruistic reasons. My buddy Pat and I were both failing in this teacher's class. One day he called us into his office, pointed a finger at each of us, and said, "You and you, you ain't fuckin' walking." He talked to us just like that: "You ain't fuckin' walking."

"Well, why'd you call us in?"

"Here's what's going to happen: Me, I enjoy my summers. I've got this little tiki hut in the backyard, and I need to add to my collection of drinks. So what you're gonna do is," he said, pointing at Pat, "you're gonna buy me a bottle of Johnnie Walker Black." He then pointed at me. "You're gonna get me a bottle of Johnnie Walker Blue. Gift wrap them. I have cafeteria in fifth period, so I won't be in my classroom. The door will be unlocked. Nobody will be in here. You come in and put the bottles in that drawer of my desk. Make sure they're gift-wrapped! That's the only way you two idiots are walking."

Johnnie Walker Blue was a premium blend, and it cost about a hundred dollars a bottle, but even if I'd had the money, I wasn't old enough to buy it. I couldn't discuss this little act of bribery with my father, especially since he and this teacher had played football together and knew each other, so I went home and had a quiet conversation with my mother.

"Listen, I'm not graduating unless I buy this guy the bottle. They keep it behind the counter because it's so expensive. I need you to get it for me."

My poor mom said, "Well, if that's what it takes . . ." She bought the bottle, and gift wrapped it for me, and I dropped it off.

As the final weeks of my senior year ticked down, and I waited to see if my "gift" to the history teacher was going to pay off, I made a conscious effort to put some distance between me and the negative influences in my life. From now on, I pledged to myself, I would stay on a productive path toward becoming a successful adult.

But, wouldn't you know it, it was right at this time that I got involved in a little "borderline" adventure with my Uncle Pete.

Pete was married to my father's sister. Over the years, he had always been more of an older brother to me than an uncle. He was a truck driver and a master mechanic, and he had lots of friends who were hardcore bikers, but he was always there to talk me through trouble, kick my ass when it was called for, and guide me back to the right path. He'd been in some tough fights of his own during his life—one time he'd been stabbed, and another time had his head caved in with a hammer—but he'd survived.

Looking back today, I have to say that if it weren't for Pete, I'd probably be dead. I say that because, as a "tenured professor" at the University of Bayonne, Pete was second to none. He had always cut a broad swath through life, but he had an unerring instinct for determining exactly where the dividing line was. He would often toe that line, and test that line, but he would never cross it. I definitely learned a lot from him.

One day I was out in front of our apartment, tinkering on a 1969 GTO I had recently bought from my aunt, when Pete pulled up. He was behind the wheel of a fully loaded black Chevy Suburban. This vehicle was totally out of reach for people in our financial stratum. I guessed he must have been doing some sort of mechanical or cosmetic work for the owner, but I joked, "Who the hell did you steal this from?"

As always, his response was quick and sarcastic: "You're a shit mechanic, and you don't know what the fuck you're doing fixing that car! I'll help you with it later. Get in and take a ride with me. I gotta go down to a house in Mantoloking." Mantoloking is a community on the Jersey shore. It is also the wealthiest borough in the state.

Whenever Uncle Pete asked me to "take a ride" with him, I always jumped at the chance. It usually meant we were going to have a blast. This was several years before Pete was diagnosed with the cancer that would eventually kill him, but he always pushed life to the edge— which was precisely why I always jumped at any chance to be his copilot.

A drive down to Mantoloking could mean just about anything, so I ducked into the house, washed up, and ran back out to join him. As soon as I jumped into the Suburban, I knew my guess that he must have been doing some cosmetic work had to be wrong. The vehicle was brand new with hardly any miles on it, and it was equipped with all the bells and whistles.

We burned through Staten Island at an unsafe speed, and then hit the Garden State Parkway. There, as always in the warmer months, it was bumper-to-bumper traffic.

As we crawled along, he said "Check this out" and opened the center console. Inside was a cellular telephone. I'd heard about them but had never actually seen one. The technology was new, and everyone was saying they would put pay phones out of business. Back then it probably cost a mortgage payment to purchase one of those phones, and God knows how much per minute to make a call. Pete picked it up and started making calls.

Pete's impatience with the traffic finally got the better of him and his recklessness kicked in. He swung out into the grass median and raced ahead to cut off as much traffic as he could. At an increasing speed, it felt like we were the feature act in a monster truck show. Dirt and grass flew each time the front of the vehicle launched off the ground and then touched down. I was laughing hysterically and fearing for my life at the same time.

With my stomach in my mouth, I blurted, "Pete! Better slow down! The owner's gonna be pissed if we crash! Whose is it anyway?"

His reply stunned me. "My boss's. It's Tony's new truck. Nice, right?"

My laughter evaporated, replaced by cold fear. Pete's boss was Tony Cherundolo. "Are you frigging kidding me? Your boss that owns the trucking company that's controlled by Johnny DiGilio's crew?"

"Yeah, don't worry. It's his company car," he replied, just before he screamed out the window at the other drivers sitting in traffic.

"You gotta slow down, man! This isn't cool. You mess this truck up and somebody's gonna kill you!"

John DiGilio had been a made member within the Genovese crime family, and he controlled the unions in the Bayonne MOTBY and the ports. He and other family members had recently been tried in federal court for racketeering offenses. DiGilio refused to retain a lawyer, and instead represented himself. He beat the charges, but his codefendants were all convicted. This had a severe impact on the Genovese control of the longshoreman's union, which was ultimately lost to the Gambino family.

Because of this, the Genovese Administration arranged for members of DiGilio's own crew to murder their boss. "Johnny Dee," as he was known, was shot and killed by two of Bayonne's very own: Louis Auricchio, the brother-in-law of a New Jersey senator, and George Weingartner, a retired Bayonne police sergeant.*

John DiGilio's body had just recently surfaced in the Hackensack River, and as I mentioned earlier, my father had shown me one of the

---

* In 1994, Auricchio confessed to the murder, pleaded guilty, and was sentenced to thirty years. Four years later, in the middle of his own trial for the murder, Weingartner committed suicide.

autopsy photos. Knowing all of this filled me with dread. I begged my uncle to slow down. After processing what I was telling him, he pulled back into traffic and we had a longer but far more relaxing drive to the house in Mantoloking.

We arrived at what to my adolescent eyes looked like a Renaissance palace. It was situated right on the water, and featured all the typical Italianate flourishes, including a fountain in the front and giant statues of lions.

Pete rang the bell. Within seconds, the huge front door opened, and standing there was a stunningly beautiful girl wearing nothing but a bikini bottom. Her simple greeting was "Hi, you guys. C'mon in."

The interior of the house was just as impressive as the outside, right down to the double Viking refrigerators and Carrara marble throughout the house. (Yes, I managed to notice all that when I wasn't gaping at the half-naked girl.)

Pete and I were greeted by his boss, Tony Cherundolo. The first thing he asked me was what I thought of his new truck. Feeling like I was about to pass out, I managed to respond, "Yeah, it's great!" He walked us out back where there was a small party going on, with gangsters and beautiful half-dressed women. They all greeted us with handshakes and smiles. My uncle seemed to know most of them, and I recognized a few faces from the neighborhood. They were all drinking, and on a table was a small bowl of cocaine that the girls seemed to be paying a lot of attention to.

After each of us had drunk a beer, I could tell my uncle realized he needed to get me out of there. If my father found out that his brother-in-law had taken me to a mob gathering, with booze, cocaine, and topless women, there was a good chance Pete would end up in the hospital.

Cherundolo ordered a couple of the goons to hoist two large coolers and stow them in the back of the Suburban. He told me to pick up a smaller cooler that was sitting nearby. I picked it up reluctantly, my mind racing with questions. *What the hell's inside this thing? Is it dope? Is it body parts?*

As we made our way outside, I was mightily relieved to hear Cherundolo explain that they'd been out on a tuna fishing trip, and the coolers were filled with the catch. He said the smaller cooler was for us, as payment for making the drive down and hauling the coolers back to Bayonne.

We drove back and delivered the large coolers without incident, and Pete dropped me off at home later that evening. As I entered our apartment, my mother asked me where I'd been. She was understandably nervous because one minute I'd been working on my car, and the next minute I'd disappeared for parts unknown with crazy Uncle Pete. I handed over several thick tuna steaks and told her the story, leaving out some of the more questionable and racy details. She was very happy to make room for the tuna in our very tiny freezer while my father, who'd been sitting there listening to my account, just rolled his eyes.

In the months that followed, every time mom cooked us up some tuna steaks, I thought about that house and those mobsters. But, most of all, I thought about all those gorgeous half-naked women.

The end of my final school year was approaching fast, and I didn't really have a plan for the future. But then a pure stroke of luck had handed me a career opportunity. One of my friends, whose father was also a cop, came to me one day and said, "New Jersey Bell is coming in to give a test to anyone who would like to work for them."

"I don't want to work for the phone company! What are you talking about?"

"Listen, man! They come in, they give us the test, and we're off for four periods. So we cut out for the rest of the day, and go get drunk, or go hang out in New York."

"Where do I sign up?"

Somebody must have been looking out for me, because not long after I sat for the test I received a call from New Jersey Bell, telling me I had passed and offering me a job. Within a week of graduation, I was enrolled at its tech school, training to be a telephone repairman. Not long after my nineteenth birthday, I was out on the road doing installation and repair.

Of course, being me, I was happy to work in the worst areas. I ended up in the ghettos in Jersey City and Greenville and the Duncan projects—bad, bad places. Some of them were so bad that the company had declared them "two-man zones." Repairmen weren't allowed to go in alone; they had to be accompanied by another employee.

As a telephone guy, I saw a lot of crazy shit, so it was probably a good thing that, by this stage of my life, very little surprised me. One time I was in Jersey City, fixing somebody's phone, and a kid came lurching into the house. He was a teenager, maybe sixteen or seventeen. He'd been shot through the back of his leg and his whole shin was blown out through the front. He was lying on the couch, bone fragments sticking out, screaming his head off, and I was telling him, "Dude, you gotta get that looked at!"

From what he was saying, I gathered he'd been shot at the corner of Forrest Street and Martin Luther King Drive. Assuming he was a corner boy—a low-end drug dealer—rivals from another corner probably came by, spraying slugs, and he caught one in the back of the leg.

This wasn't my first rodeo. If the gun thugs came looking for him, I didn't want to be there. So I left.

On other occasions, drug dealers tried to pay me to hook them up with an illegal phone line. Guys from Duncan projects, heavy-duty drug suppliers, would say to me, "I'll give you $3,000 if you hook up a phone. Tap me into any line, hook me up, let me do my deals."

I'd have to talk my way out of that. When I told them "I'm not going to do that," they'd get pissed off, and I'd have to calm them down. It was a good thing that I had learned the hard way, growing up on the street, how to de-escalate dangerous situations.

That skill was especially valuable when I had to deal with the old-school Italian mob guys who were constantly demanding to see my work orders, making sure I wasn't putting in a tap. One time, I was on a pole in an Italian neighborhood, in the middle of repairs, and a fat guy came out of a social club and called me down. "Get down off the fuckin' pole!" he yelled.

I looked down. "Get out of here! Who are you?"

"Come down here!"

"Fuck you!" I was skinny, strong, and wiry in those days, and a bit too cocky.

A few other guys came out and joined him. He yelled, "I'm telling you right now, you better get your ass down off that pole!"

So I climbed down and was immediately surrounded by these wiseguys.

"Give me your fuckin' work order!" I showed it to them. Then it was "You see any wiretaps up there? Anywhere around here, for that matter? You seen any, kid?"

"No."

"You ever see anything, you let us know. Understand?"

"Yeah. Of course."

In those days, the feds used to hardwire their taps. I saw them all the time. So, yes, they were there, but I wasn't saying anything. I wasn't that stupid.

Eventually the day came when I decided to sit for the police examination.

I had always looked up to my father. Although I'd spent most of my growing-up years hanging out with bad kids and getting into capers, I'd always known when to stop. I'd be tempting fate, doing those things, but when it was over I'd always feel a gnawing regret.

There was a lot of racial tension when we were kids, but if I called somebody a racist name, I always felt terrible afterward. I'd be telling myself, *That's not you. That's not the person you want to be. You're better than this.* I never shared those thoughts with my cronies, but I would lie awake on a lot of nights struggling with myself, struggling with my behavior.*

I remember the day when I first thought I wanted to be a cop. I was twelve years old, and our parents had taken us to the Hudson Mall, in Jersey City, to see *Raiders of the Lost Ark*. As we were driving home in

---

* As an adult, I've always tried to raise my kids differently from what I saw when I was growing up. I don't want them to have hate in their hearts for anyone. I don't want them to see people for the color of their skin or their religious beliefs. I just want them to understand that there are good people and bad people and they need to always be watchful.

my parents' '76 Impala, with my sister, brother, and me in the backseat, my father recognized a man standing on the side of the road. There was a warrant out for the guy, and the police had been searching for him for a long time. Dad knew there was usually a squad car stationed near the borderline between Jersey City and Bayonne, so he pulled in and briefed the young cop who was sitting there. Then he jumped into the squad car, and they left us sitting there as they raced back to grab the guy. As I learned later, when the fugitive started sprinting away, my father yelled, "If you keep running, I'm going to shoot you in the back."

The guy stopped, put his hands up, and said, "All right, Lenny."

That's how it was. That's how much even the bad guys respected my father.

Dad came back, with the guy in cuffs in the back of the squad car, and told my mom, "Follow us to the precinct. I'm just going to process him real fast and write up a quick arrest report, and I'll be right out."

Watching my father make that arrest was all it took. Until then, I had never seen him in action where he transformed from dad mode to cop mode and took somebody into custody. It made me want to be a cop like him. Of course, I didn't bother to tell him my little secret for quite a few more years—I was too busy failing at school and hanging out with delinquents.

After I'd been at the phone company for a few years, my father told me the department was recruiting. He suggested I take the test. I did, and I passed it. One evening he said, "The chief will be calling you tonight. They're hiring ten officers, and he's willing to make an eleventh spot for you, if you want the job."

I had scored pretty high on the test, but not high enough to be offered one of the ten openings. However, the chief in question respected my father and my family—one of my grandfathers had also been a cop—so he was willing to create an extra spot for me. He was doing it for my father more than for me.

Even then, I had a hard time letting go of my habit of pretending not to care about anything. When the phone call came in, the chief said, "Look, I'm willing to create an eleventh spot for you, if that's what you want. Do you want this job?"

I said, "Yeah. OK. Sure."

"Well, you better be a little more convincing than that."

"Yeah, of course I want the job. I might have to take a cut in pay, but sure, I want to be a cop. Why not?"

Obviously that offhand reply didn't exactly inspire confidence, so he shot back, "Listen, you're going to have to show me more than that."

They decided to send me to the Jersey City Police Academy. Thank God it was to Jersey City because, with my attitude, I would have failed any other academy. As you might have guessed, I didn't do well with rules.

The Jersey City Police Academy was much more laid back than most. The instructors didn't worry so much about how many jumping jacks you could do, how you stood at attention, or the creases in your pants. They taught you how to be a street cop and survive. One of the best examples I can offer is this: A salty old instructor stood in front of us and said, "All right, today I'm going to teach report-writing. We're going to go over how to write a police report, how to organize it, and what to focus on. But, before we get into that . . . everybody, look at me. Pay attention now!" He picked up a flashlight—one of the old three-cell battery Maglites. "See this here?" He held it up. "See this? This is the end that the batteries go in. And this is the end where the light comes out. OK? Got that? Now . . . when you hit somebody with this, you hold it by the end where the lightbulb is! Understand? Because these lightbulbs cost five to seven dollars to replace! You always hit the guy with the battery end, the heavier end. OK? You all got that? All right. Now I'm going to teach you how to write a report."

You wouldn't get that anywhere else. The Jersey City Police Academy taught each of us how to be a tough cop in a tough precinct. The instructors taught us how to be empathetic when it counts and hard-assed when it counts. We learned from seasoned Jersey City police officers and top homicide investigators—the best of the best. I consider myself most fortunate to have been trained by these guys. They helped immeasurably in preparing me for my career down the road. And, years later, I was lucky enough to conduct investigations with some of my former instructors—working side by side with the same cops I had looked up to when I was a green recruit.

At the age of twenty-two, I graduated from the academy and was back on the streets—and raring to go.

4

BACK ON THE STREETS

AS A ROOKIE OFFICER, I was mostly working nights. But night shift was where the action was, and I was loving it.

I have an especially fond memory of one night patrol. I was dispatched to a bar fight—and who was the bartender? My twelfth-grade history teacher. He didn't have a license to work behind the bar, and New Jersey state law requires bartenders to be licensed. He was just doing it for extra money.

I walked in, and he didn't recognize me. I asked a few questions and then banged him with five tickets, each carrying a pretty hefty fine. He couldn't believe it.

"What am I getting all these for?"

"Read the bottom of the ticket."

"What am I looking for?"

"Read the name."

He read the name, and I said, "I don't forget," and left with a grin on my face.

I tried to model myself after my father, who had instructed me, "Be your own man, and be an honest cop and be a good cop. Always try to do the right thing. Treat people the way you'd want to be treated. And don't ever let me hear that you beat up somebody who was handcuffed." That was one of the things that always irked my father—cops beating up on people who couldn't defend themselves. I saw a few cops do stuff like that, and they disgusted me as much as they disgusted my dad.

I loved the job. I worked patrol, and right out of the gate I was hungry for action. I hooked up with a cop named Timmy, who ended up being my partner for nearly ten years. He was a big guy, six feet and change, and pure muscle. We made a great team, and over the years we made easily over a thousand arrests together. In the realm of violent police work, there was very little we didn't experience. Sometimes we ended up literally fighting for our lives, and for each other's lives. I couldn't have picked a better partner and best friend.

It will come as no surprise that Timmy and I soon had a reputation on the street. Certain cops pull up—not just me and Timmy but also some other guys in the department—and they are known. If people screwed with us, they'd get hurt. If they saw us get out of a car, they had to get their shit together real quick. I know how that sounds, but because I carried myself the way my father had told me to, I gained some of the same respect he had enjoyed. That made it easier to defuse violent situations.

Timmy and I were an aggressive team, as were some of the other cops on our shift. Almost every night we had some kind of action going on, and we did a lot of pursuits. It got to the point where we were getting yelled at by some of the bosses—crabby old cops who told us, "Knock it off! Don't start another damned pursuit tonight! I need my sleep!"

Eventually, after about two years on the job, the situation reached a breaking point. During a late-night pursuit, some cops got into an accident and people got hurt. I wasn't personally involved, but shortly after that—out of the blue—I was sent to the New Jersey State Police narcotics investigation school. There was even talk around the department that I might get a gold detective's shield.

The reason soon became clear. One night, our shift captain told Timmy and me, "You know what? Thank God you guys are getting made detectives. As soon as you go out through those doors and you go down that hall and you start working as detectives, don't ever fuckin' come back here! You don't belong on patrol; stay down there!"

I did "stay down there." After completing the narcotics course, I was assigned to an organized crime task force—but, to my disappointment, it was a Vice operation. I had wanted Narcotics, but that unit was full, so I ended up on day shift, working old time gangsters—old school bookie guys. I thought the work would be boring, but it wasn't. I worked some really good cases and enjoyed the assignment. But after a short stint on that task force, I ended up right where I'd wanted to be: on Narcotics and back on nights.

And then came the turning point in my career.

5

TFO

ONE MORNING, I showed up at work riding a 1977 Harley Davidson motorcycle. The chopper belonged to my Uncle Pete, but he would let me borrow it whenever I wanted. I was dressed in uniform pants, a white T-shirt, and a leather vest. I don't know what the hell I was thinking, doing that, and my chief didn't appreciate it at all. When I pulled in, he was standing there, and he realized it was me. Back then you didn't have cops like you have now—weekend warriors with tattoos that they think make them tough. In those days, the only acceptable tattoos were military. You were either a good guy or a bad guy. No good guy wanted to be a biker, but I still had that in me.

The chief was royally pissed. "What the fuck you doing on this bike? Are you crazy? I gave you this job!" He ripped me a new one and stormed off.

But he must have thought about it, because three weeks later he called me in and asked if I'd be interested in doing some kind of undercover gig.

I said, "Yeah, no problem."

"Well, don't get too cocky about it!"

"You know who I am, Chief," I said. "You know how I used to be. Whatever you need done, I'll do it."

From that point on, I was in. I started out doing short stints of undercover (UC) work while I was on the Narcotics squad—just dabbling in it. But after a time, I was asked to join a DEA task force, and I ended up working several DEA operations over a number of years. But even though I was now a local law enforcement officer assigned to a federal task force—a TFO (task force officer), as they called us—I never received any official undercover training. The "tradecraft" I was using, if it could be graced with that term, was entirely self-taught, just whatever I had picked up on the street as a neighborhood kid or working at the phone company, or from other UCs I had met on the job.

Because of my lack of training, I made a lot of operational mistakes during the first few years and almost got myself killed. Eventually, a particularly dangerous DEA operation put me in a situation where I was at serious risk of losing my life. By then I was married with two young children, so I decided to step back. I gave up UC operations and returned to working major cases in the detective bureau.

My determination to play it safe didn't last long. After I'd worked on a couple of homicide investigations, our chief retired. Soon after, the new chief called me in to a closed-door meeting. He said, "Listen, we've got some organized crime problems that are tied into the department. We've got some cops dealing drugs. I want to see if you'd be interested in spearheading an investigation."

I said, "Yeah, no problem," which was pretty much my answer to everything.

He let me pick my own team—two other cops that I trusted. We used rental cars and communicated with those little walkie-talkie radios that kids play with. At one point, we partnered up with a federal task force, and I found myself working side by side with some FBI agents.

In the course of that case, we ended up targeting some guys who had hijacked a truckload of bedsheets and were selling them off through a tanning salon owned by the mob. The feds wanted somebody to go in and make a buy, so I said I'd do it. We had no ops plan; it was completely off the cuff. I parked my car outside the business, went in, did the deal, and came out. It was a piece of cake, but Mark, one of the agents I was working with, was pretty impressed. He told me he wanted to introduce me to his friend Pino at the FBI, who was running some undercover operations. I learned later that he had already spoken about me to Pino, telling him he really should meet this cop from Hudson County, that we would really hit it off. Pino's initial response had been "No way. Hudson County's too corrupt. There's so much corruption in the police departments over there you don't know who to trust. I don't want to meet him."

But Mark was persistent, and eventually Pino agreed to have me come in. As I entered the office, I was met by a guy who immediately reminded me of Joe Pesci—short in stature, but with a presence and a confidence that dominated the room. There was nothing of the FBI shirt-and-tie conventionality about this guy. Within minutes of shaking Pino's hand, I knew we were going to be friends. The UC mentality, the mannerisms, the shared understanding—it was plain that we would be a good match.

Before I could officially join the FBI's LCN (La Cosa Nostra) Task Force, I would be required to undergo a certain level of training. Pino said, "I can't just let you do undercover work for the Bureau without assessing you. Have you ever had any formal training?"

"No."

"OK, I'm going to send you to school. I'll tell you what . . . I can slide you into a UC school I'm hosting for guys who want to be undercover certified."

"Sounds good."

He was as good as his word, and I was quickly enrolled in the UC course. I learned a lot there—understanding complex human interactions and other factors I'd never taken into consideration as a self-taught undercover officer. The instructors provided me with a great foundation, teaching me some effective techniques and forcing me to reevaluate the way I operated. I came to the cold realization that I'd been doing a lot of things all wrong.

When it was over, I told Pino, "That course was good. I could do this full time."

He said, "Giovanni, let's get you settled on the task force, and then I want to get you signed up for the FBI's undercover school. It's like this class you just finished, but on steroids. That way, you'll become a certified FBI undercover, and you could work any case, anywhere."

I jumped at the chance.

But soon after, Pino came back to me. "I'm getting some push-back from the FBI higher-ups. They think you've had too many years doing this stuff and that you're too set in your old ways."

Knowing this was a critical moment in my law enforcement career, my response to him was heated. "Pino, I'm at the stage in my career where I'm starting to take other people into undercover jobs with me. I'm worried I'm going to get somebody hurt or even killed. One day I'm going to retire from this job, and I'm gonna want to teach—in fact, I'm already teaching some the younger guys how to do this. But because *I* don't have any formal training, that means *they* don't have any formal training. I don't want to be retired, sitting on a lounge chair somewhere, and I hear that one of the kids I worked with was killed because I taught him how to do something the wrong way. I don't want to live with that on my conscience. The FBI needs to give me a chance!"

Pino believed in me, and he proved it by going back to the Bureau and pitching my case again. This time the bosses agreed to let me take a shot.

After an initial battery of psychological and behavioral evaluations, I was given the green light to join the next class. I admit that I was seriously anxious going in. The program was widely known for being extremely intense. I'd heard that members of outside agencies, who had attended previous classes as observers, had commented that people had to be crazy to subject themselves to an ordeal like that for weeks on end.

But I was determined to see it through, and it didn't take long for me to realize that the level of training I was exposed to was going to be invaluable. Just the psychological end of covert operations was a revelation. The amount of preparation and planning for each level of an operation has to be thorough and painstaking because, in the criminal underworld, you could be double-crossed at any moment.

It wasn't just classroom sessions. There were also role-playing scenarios, which were a completely new training vehicle for me. The planners try to keep the playing field consistent for all candidates based on their previous UC experience. In other words, the planners throw them into unfamiliar roles to see how they handle stress and palpable danger.

I was mostly comfortable with this stuff, so I was doing well. But then, in one of my classes, the instructor started talking about intelligence operations. I had no clue about that world. I was a drug guy, a stolen-property guy, a guy who made street buys. Sometimes, I was the guy who did the murder-for-hire gig. I said to myself, *OK, I can do this. It'll be a blast.* But the problem with intelligence/counterintelligence is that your associates can be far more highly educated and refined than you or the people you'd been dealing with over the years.

But I had an ace up my sleeve. His name was Eddie Sanchez.

To explain, I'll need to rewind slightly. I had been instructed to report to a specific offsite location. When I walked into my room, I discovered that I'd been assigned a roommate. Another candidate was already there, unpacking his luggage. When I keyed the door and walked in, he was just as surprised as I was.

He introduced himself, saying "Hi, I'm Eddie," as he removed a Bible from his luggage and placed it on the bedside table.

"Hey, Eddie. How you doin'? I'm Giovanni. What's with the Bible? You know that's not gonna help you here, right? From what I hear, we're pretty screwed!"

He chuckled and responded, "Who knows? It could just save us both."

Over the following days, in addition to regular classroom sessions, we were assigned to a string of role-playing scenarios. These required us to negotiate serious criminal deals, handle surprise crises, and even negotiate for each other's lives. It didn't help our performances that we were persistently—and no doubt deliberately—sleep deprived.

As the training ramped up, trainees started dropping like flies. Some left after sustaining physical injuries, but the majority decamped because they couldn't handle the mental stressors. In the face of all this, Eddie and I formed a close bond with each other and with Jack, another task force officer from Hawaii. Because of our experiences together, the three of us became like long-lost brothers, always watching each other's backs.

Eddie himself came from an intelligence background, but that hadn't prepared him for situations like negotiating large narcotic deals or dealing with white supremacists or violent street gangs. Unlike Jack and me, Eddie was not a street kid by any means, and he started to worry that he wouldn't graduate.

But after making it into this school, which was a high-water mark in UC training, failure was simply not an option. All three of us had left our families back home for weeks, and we were determined to pass. So we made a pact and started a program of "cross-training." Jack and I used our small amount of spare time to give Eddie crash courses in how to survive in the underworld. He was like a sponge and soaked up everything we taught him. And it worked both ways. When we came to the intelligence portion of the program, both Jack and I were just too "street" for James Bond work. So during other late-night sessions, Eddie gave us crash courses on how to handle ourselves regarding intelligence work.

The fact that I had so many years of doing successful undercover work prior to my "official training" made me a prime target for instructors and management to "amp up" the training modules to test my abilities. I don't blame them for this. In their position, I would have done the same.

I was briefed by my counselor, Steve, who handed me a recording device and emphasized that it was imperative that I wear it. In the meantime, unknown to me, the two instructors who had been cast as my "adversaries" in the pending setup had been told that I would be wearing a wire. The plan was to intensify the action by ensuring that the opposing players would quickly find the device and everything would go horribly wrong for me. The point was to see if I had the experience to survive in such a situation. In other words, the instructors had deliberately set me up to fail.

I was basically a lamb headed to the slaughter.

I headed to the arranged meeting and knocked on the door. It swung open, and two guys dressed in suits were standing there—both big, imposing individuals. They looked like Russian gangsters.

One of them said, "Yeah? Who're you?"

"I'm Johnnie." I was already feeling out of place, dressed in jeans and a biker-style T-shirt with skulls all over it.

"Hey, Johnnie! How are you doing? Why don't you come in?"

As soon as I stepped into the room, it was on! They pinned me up against the door and start patting me down.

"Hey, get your fuckin' hands off me! What're ya doin'?"

This guy started grabbing at me, pulling at my pants.

"What the hell? What's your fuckin' deal?"

"Just checking—make sure you're not wearing."

"What? You wanna to check me for a wire or something?" Right then, I decided to slide full bore into survival mode. "Here . . . you know what? Let me save you the trouble!" And I started pulling my pants down. I mean, *right down*. The two goons backed away.

"Whoa, whoa, what are you doin'?"

"Well, obviously you wanna grab at me and open my pants, so let's get down to it! I've been in lockup before. I know the drill. What's your fuckin' problem?"

The one guy said, "Pick your pants up."

Of course, as instructed, I was wearing the recording device my handler had provided. It was in my pants, and they never found it. So, after their abortive search, they asked me to sit down. I complied, and their boss entered the room.

At this point, one of the enforcers pulled out a gun. "Don't move!"

I stayed calm. "Buddy, look at the size of you guys. There's no reason for a gun. I ain't gonna hurt you."

"It's just in case, just in case."

"Just in case? In case of what? You searched me, I ain't got a gun on me, but hell, you want to hold a gun? Hold a gun if it makes you feel better. But the two of you guys—I promise you, I'm not going to kick the shit out of you. I can't."

Without giving up too many training details, I can tell you that I walked out of that scenario completely unscathed.

Immediately after, I was taken before the panel of observers for a debriefing session. In my case, two female UC mentors had been assigned to debrief me. And, as it turned out, one of these women was not the biggest fan of "that cop from New Jersey."

They began by asking me to explain my goals, objectives, and the instructions that I had received from management. I did so, and then one of them started questioning my understanding of the instruction to wear a recording device. During the next few minutes, she glared and snarled at me as if I was a ten-year-old. "Was it explained to you that management had instructed that you were to be equipped with a recording device?"

"Yes."

"So you understood that it was *imperative* for operational and intelligence purposes?"

She was behaving like a defense attorney, thinking she was chasing me down a rabbit hole. I knew exactly where she was going, so I baited her.

"Yes, I did."

"The role players did not locate a device on you after they searched you. Is that correct?"

"Yes."

"Why is that?" she asked, in an increasingly accusatory tone. "Did you even have it with you? Or did you not follow the directions you were given?"

"I followed the directions, and I did have it with me."

Her eyes widened as if she was now absolutely certain she was about to hand me my ass. "I find it *very* hard to believe that these two guys searched you and missed it! I don't believe you followed the instructions. So, where is that device right now? Did you leave it somewhere outside after your counselor gave it to you?"

My counselor was in the room with us, sitting quietly to one side. I looked over to him, as if to ask, "What the hell is with her?"

He wore a look of profound disappointment. He knew he would not be able to help me if I had ditched the recording device. If I had, the best that could happen was that I would be dinged points. More likely, I would fail the program.

I should explain that counselors at the school take personal pride in their candidates' successes, and there was an informal competition among them to produce the best graduate. In a sense, they viewed themselves as scouts, or talent agents, looking for the next great performer to give them bragging rights within the veteran community. Throughout the course, Steve had been the assigned counselor for me, Jack, and Eddie. He was an experienced operative, and he had mentored us closely, strongly believing in our ability to do great things. For that reason, and quite apart from my own personal stress at the prospect of failing this class, I couldn't bear the thought of letting him down.

Seeing his downcast expression, I shot him a look that said, *It's OK, boss. I got this.*

Politely and respectfully, I responded to my overheated cross-examiner: "No, ma'am, I did not leave the device outside. I followed the instructions and took it into the scenario with me."

"Oh, really?" she shot back. "If that's the case, where is the device right at this very moment? Go get it and give it to us!"

"I still have it on me. Do you want it right now?"

"You're telling us you have it on you right now? If that is the case, give it to me, *now!*"

"Well, if you want it, I'm OK giving it to you." I rose from my seat. "Just let me reach into my pants and get it."

Everyone in the room had been watching the last few minutes of this little drama unfold like a bad soap opera. But, hearing that response, they all realized that I was about to throw down my cards like a seasoned poker player. I could feel the room start to rally behind me. As I began to reach into my pants to retrieve the device, I glanced over at Steve. Seeing the look of triumph on my face, he gave me an expression that told me he was shrieking on the inside with pride and delight.

The inquisitor's face was a portrait of utter humiliation. Sticking it to her in front of her peers was worth every second of this parody. She quickly ended our debriefing session and dismissed me from the room.

Outside, Steve rushed up to me wearing a huge smile. "Fucking A, Johnny man! You scared me there for a minute!"

I held out the device. "Do you want this?"

"Hell, no! I'm not touching that thing after it was almost in your ass! Give it to the techs and go back to your room. I'll come and get you later. Great job!"

Steve remains one of the most respected covert operatives I have ever known, and I will be forever grateful to him. He is now right where he deserves to be: retired and playing golf full time.

In the end, Eddie, Jack, and I all successfully completed the training and headed into the operational underworld.

It was that FBI course in general, and that role-playing scenario in particular, that gave me the confidence to believe I could work any operation in any situation. Immediately after graduation, I began my career as an FBI undercover TFO. It felt very good to know that, whatever came up, I was certified to be operational, whether a case involved drugs, money laundering, murder for hire, intelligence, terrorism . . . whatever they needed.

And as for Pino, who had made it all possible, I will never forget the very first case I worked on with him. He was involved with some Dominican drug traffickers, and the operation was already underway when he recruited me to help. As he explained it, he had recently taken a meeting with the group's boss. But after that meeting, the boss and a few members of his crew had gotten themselves into an argument with some thugs in New York. The boss ended up putting eight rounds into one of them and had been arrested. Pino asked me to join him and two other operatives at a dinner with a couple of the Dominican boss's subordinates.

Using my undercover identity of "Giovanni Gatto," I tagged along. Pino pretty much led the discussion, and the other operatives chimed in from time to time. I have to admit I was a bit nervous. I guess you could say I saw this as the "big stage," and I was struck with opening-night jitters. I didn't want to inject myself into the conversation and end up saying something stupid.

The talk was mainly social, focused on baseball and hockey. One of our targets explained how he used to love to play hockey until he'd broken his femur. The table went quiet for a second—I guess because everyone was thinking about the unreal pain the guy must have experienced (or, maybe, trying to think of how many Dominican hockey teams they'd ever heard of). It was then that I decided to speak up.

Very casually, I said, "That's the hardest bone in the body to break."

All eyes turned to me.

Pino asked, "What did you say, Giovanni?"

"Uh, nothing, Pino. Just saying . . . that's the hardest bone in the body to break."

"How the hell do you know that? Did you learn that in med school? Are you a fuckin' doctor and I didn't know?"

Everyone laughed at his joke, including the targets. I immediately realized what he was doing, so I played along. "Naw, I ain't no fucking doctor, Pino. But I can tell you that when some fucker owes your boss money, and he don't pay up, the femur is the hardest bone in the body. I know that because I hit them with a fuckin' baseball bat until I'm outta breath and my arms get tired."

Pino really played on that, laughing loudly in the restaurant. "You motherfucker, Giovanni! I fuckin' love it! That's why I'm glad you're with me, you sick fuck! I love dis guy!"

The targets looked on in disbelief as Pino and I laughed together like two sinister sociopaths, discussing in great detail what Giovanni was willing to do on behalf of his pal Pino. The fearful, aghast looks on their faces were utterly priceless.

I guess you could say that was the precise moment when the underworld persona of Giovanni Gatto was born.

6

HOME FIRES

By now, it is probably obvious that my police career was no ordinary one. And, as it happens, my family is no ordinary family.

I met my wife Anna in 2001 when I was working with the DEA on a Mexican drug cartel case. It was a huge investigation centered in New York and New Jersey, consuming almost every waking hour of my day, seven days a week. For most of the operation, I was living in a hotel room provided by the DEA. Our group was up on a couple of wiretaps and was waiting for a big shipment of coke to come in from Mexico.

Some of the action was taking place in a New Jersey county just outside Manhattan where Anna was a police detective. Her agency was mainly providing surveillance support, and at one point in the operation, when I was out in the field, I needed a couple of radios and some fresh batteries. The radios enabled us to communicate with all the different police agencies we had working with us. I tried to enlist someone to pick up the equipment from the female cop who'd been assigned to deliver it, but nobody was available. So, reluctantly and feeling pissed off, I got in my car and ripped down the highway to the McDonald's restaurant where she was waiting. I'd been given her cell phone number, so I called her up, sounding a bit abrupt, and said, "Yeah, I'm here. I'm in the Mustang. Just pass them off to me. Thanks."

At this point in my life, I was in the process of separating from my first wife, with whom I had a daughter and a son. My wife and I still had a relationship—not a physical relationship, but one that was primarily focused on the kids. She knew I wouldn't be moving back into our house when the case was over, and it was understood between us that we would be getting a divorce. As far as I was concerned, I was going to be a single guy again, with periodic access to my kids. It wasn't going to be the most ideal situation for any of us, but I thought it was necessary for our collective well-being.

I had always sworn I wouldn't date a female cop, and that I would never, under any circumstances, have an ongoing relationship with a female cop. So nothing in particular was on my mind that day except to take custody of a couple of radios and a handful of batteries.

Yes, I know what you're thinking—and you're right. We hear about this all the time, and it sounds like such a cliché, but here it is: I got out of my car in that McDonald's parking lot, took one look at Detective Anna, and that was it. I was smitten. I was done. I don't know what happened, but she had me before she said hello.

The investigation we were working on became one of the most successful the New Jersey DEA ever undertook. We seized twenty-five hundred kilos of cocaine and around $4 million in cash. And because Anna had been assigned to help us with surveillance, she and I ended up connecting out in the field a few times and having a few laughs together. Then one night, I just came right out and asked her: "You know, when we finish up here, if you want, we could go get a drink. Or maybe something to eat?" That was pretty much how it started, and our relationship became more and more serious as the weeks went by.

And then came September 11, 2001—and we became inseparable.

By September of that year, I had been introduced to Anna's mother but not to her father. He was a senior law enforcement officer who was concerned about his daughter dating a cop from Hudson County. He had investigated many organized crime figures in that area in the 1970s and '80s, and he knew the neighborhoods I came from. Many of his investigations focused on people from my area and some of the cops I had worked with. From his point of view, this was reason to be suspicious of me. Nevertheless, Anna's mother, realizing that her daughter and I were serious about our relationship, finally prevailed upon him to meet me.

On Sunday, September 9, Anna and I arranged to meet her parents for lunch at a festival that was being held in Chester, Pennsylvania. Unfortunately, when we arrived we discovered that the festival grounds were completely packed and all of the restaurants had long waits. Not only did our lunchtime get-together never happen, but because we had parked at opposite ends of the crowded festival, I didn't meet her father at all. Upon both parties discovering that the eateries were all full and had long waiting lists, the four of us agreed by cell phone to catch a meal together on another day.

I was really looking forward to finally meeting her father, but that day never came.

At the time, I was living in my old neighborhood, in a small apartment that belonged to my parents. On the morning of Tuesday, September 11, I walked down the street to get a haircut. I'd been going to these two barbers, Vito and Tony, since I was five years old, and their shop was only a couple of blocks from the apartment. I got there early, just as they opened, and settled into Vito's chair. They had the TV on, and as Vito was cutting my hair, one of them suddenly exclaimed, "Hey! Look at this! A plane just crashed into the towers!"

We were all still staring at the screen, completely astounded, when the second plane hit.

Immediately, I knew. I just *knew*, and my heart sank. Two planes were not a coincidence. I told Vito to finish up quickly because I had to get to my office.

I sprinted to my car and within three minutes of leaving the shop, I was barreling up Route 440. From there, I could see the towers burning. Then, as I pulled into the parking garage under the Newark DEA building, a woman on the radio started yelling, *"The building came down! The building came down!"* I parked and raced upstairs to my office. Just as I arrived at my desk, my father called me. He was a nervous wreck, because he thought I might have been over in Manhattan. And then Anna called me, saying, "I can't get in touch with my father! He's in the area of the Trade Center. I'm going over! I've gotta go over there!"

"Calm down," I said. "Listen, let's just figure this out. I'm over here in my office in Newark. I'm with the feds now, so I'll know everything as it comes in! Let's just figure this out for a couple of minutes."

But she was adamant. "Listen, I've been trying to call my father! I can't find my father!"

As I was talking to her, one of the agents shouted, "*Holy shit! The other building's coming down!*" As I jumped up out of my seat and saw the second tower collapse to the ground, our cell service died. The cell tower on the second building was the one we used.

Almost instantly, Anna called me back on the landline. Now she was utterly frantic.

"Don't worry," I said. "Let me figure this out. As soon as they have the command center set up, I'll call there and I'll get a hold of him and I'll let you know where he is. But you know, he's a senior officer. There's no way he's going to be in those buildings."

"No, no! There's something wrong! You don't know my father! I've got to get to his office! I'm going to find him from there."

There was no talking her out of it, so I said, "All right. I'm leaving the DEA building now. I'll meet you at the rest area on the New Jersey Turnpike. I'll pick you up there."

I left the building quickly. Newark is usually packed with traffic, but when I got out on the turnpike, it felt like some movie where I was the last man on the planet. There wasn't a civilian car on the highway or a plane in the sky. It was just me and a state trooper. I raced up to the rest area, picked up Anna, and headed for her father's office. When we got there, her dad's colleagues ushered us into his office right away. I could tell they were a little freaked out themselves because they couldn't find him either.

We sat there for a while, and then in came Bobby, an inspector who was directly subordinate to Anna's father. The two men weren't just coworkers, they were close friends. Bobby was a total mess, both physically and emotionally. He was covered with dirt and soot. He didn't seem to realize it, but his suit jacket was in tatters. He tried to compose himself for the sake of Anna, but I could see in his eyes that he was deeply afraid because he couldn't find his boss and dear friend.

"We're going to find your dad," he promised Anna. "But right now, it's a lot of chaos out there. We have no communications. We're getting them back up now. We have the first wave of people coming in now, so just hang out here, and as soon as we regroup, I'll get back in here and brief you." He gave us a radiophone and promised to call us if he heard anything.

After sitting there a little longer, we heard some commotion outside and went to investigate. The first wave of employees from the collapsed buildings were arriving. We helped a couple of them settle in the office area. Some were cut up, and a lot were bruised and burned and covered with soot and debris. These people weren't cops. They were civilians who worked in the towers. Some of them were trying to rally up a team to go back to the scene and look for their coworkers, but that never happened, because the perimeter had been shut down except for emergency service vehicles.

As Anna paced around, she was getting more and more agitated. She kept looking at the pictures in her dad's office, taking it all in, soaking in the fact that they couldn't find him, and intermittently bursting into tears. The transmissions over the radio didn't help. A lot of the first responders sounded completely demoralized. One of them kept saying, "What the fuck are we doing here? What's our mission here? What the fuck are we doing?"

A lieutenant got on the radio and ordered him to maintain radio discipline. "Help those who you can! Treat those who you can! If not, let's just try to process the scene." He was barking out these orders mainly to keep these guys grounded, but one's response was "What are you talking about, LT? They're all dead!"

"Maintain radio discipline!" the supervisor yelled.

And the guy repeated, "But, LT, they're all fucking dead! It's all body parts and dead people! There's nobody here to help!"

I switched off the radio real fast, but too late, because by then Anna had completely lost it. Bobby popped his head back in, but he wasn't much help. He was doing everything he could to appear calm, for her sake, but his eyes were welling and his voice was cracking. He grabbed her and held her, whispering over and over, "We'll find him! We'll find him!" He was trying to console her, but I think he knew in his heart that there was a good chance that Anna's father was gone.

That's because—now it all started to come out—Anna's dad had been in the second tower.

As we now know, when her father received the call, he guessed right away what was happening. Years before this, he had realized that terrorism was the wave of the future, and he'd been pushing law enforcement agencies to be prepared for those investigations. He had also been personally involved in a lot of international training on the subject. When the American Airlines Flight 11 hit the north tower, he was in his vehicle, on his way to work. He immediately called ahead, advising his staff that he was heading for the scene. By agreement, he stopped at the office and picked up a few of the higher-ranking officers who wanted to go with him. By the time they arrived at the World Trade Center, United Airlines Flight 175 had struck the south tower. Without hesitation, they all headed into that building.

Some of the men who had been in the car with Anna's father survived and later shared their story of what happened next. As they were entering the building, bodies were hitting the ground all around them. As the world knows, people were jumping to their deaths. These men further explained that when they ran into Tower 2, the alarms were going off, the stairways were filled with smoke, and first responders were running everywhere. As they continued up the stairs, conditions deteriorated drastically. Many of the people coming down the stairwells had suffered from severe burns and lacerations, and some were soaked in jet fuel.

Somewhere above the sixtieth floor, Anna's father ordered the rest of his team back down the stairs to keep the flow of escaping people moving. He told them, "I'll be down in a second. I'm just going one more floor up." A few insisted on staying with him, but his response was "*I'm ordering you to move downstairs!* Keep those people moving, slow and calm. Get them out and get them away from the building. I'll be right down."

That was the last they saw of him. By giving that order, he had saved their lives, and lost his own.

In my memory, the following week is just a blur of heartbreak and horror. Anna and I spent days searching every makeshift hospital and infirmary in Manhattan. We hooked up with two of her cousins, both NYPD officers, and rode around with them like Italian gangsters, butting in at the front end of every lineup, snatching clipboards away from any nurse or doctor that was holding one, poring over every patient list, praying we'd find her father's name. When it wasn't there, we would move on to the next facility. The recovery teams kept assuring us that they had hundreds of guys out looking for him, but we trusted no one and refused to take *no* for an answer. We went out and combed the city ourselves. This was at a time when everybody was out searching, posting family members' photos on message boards and showing their faces on the news.

At one of the last places on our list, we were escorted into a small cafeteria area. We were sitting at a lunch table, and a doctor came in and he asked who we were. After Anna explained, he took her to one side and said, "Listen, I'm sorry. I really am. But because of the extreme heat, because that jet fuel was burning so intensely, in a lot of cases there are no remains. They're never going to be found."

Even though she already knew that, hearing those words spoken out loud, in that moment, was just too much, just too horrifying. Anna completely broke down. Seeing this, one of her cousins tensed up, as if he was about to lunge. Wisely, he stopped himself, but for a fleeting moment it looked like he was about to put the doctor in a chokehold.

Back in the car, everyone realized that our search was over. Anna was forced to face that cruel reality, and it was a terrible thing to see.

Like so many other victims on that day, not a trace of Anna's father has ever been found.

As days became weeks, I remained at Anna's side. Whatever her mother and the rest of the family needed to do, I was there to help—to drive them somewhere, to stand in line for them, or to undertake any of the stressful, and at times maddening, errands and duties that followed the tragedy. Whether those joint experiences had something to do with fusing our relationship I cannot say. I'm just too close to it all. All I can say is that, for me, it was Anna I wanted to be with and no other. Eventually my first wife and I divorced, and Anna and I became engaged. After we married, we were quickly blessed with a daughter and, a few years later, with a son.

But 9/11 didn't end there. For Anna, it could never end. After she went back to work, she was forced to drive the New Jersey Turnpike every day and see that empty space in the New York skyline. She had to see those black columns of smoke—that burning debris, burning for months—that marked the exact spot where her father had spent his last moments on this earth. Each day on the turnpike reopened that grievous wound. We had a rule in our house: we never went to work on September 11. We always took the day off and went to the city, to the World Trade Center site. We did things like that with her mother or just by ourselves.

Eventually, as more time passed, we got away from visiting the site on the anniversary, because it all just became too raw. Instead, we would just spend a quiet day with the kids. But then, one September, years later, Anna said to me, "Hell! You know what? I'm running out of vacation days, and I can't take another one. I'm just going to go to work." So she did—and ended up rear-ending some guy on the turnpike. She just hadn't been paying attention because she saw that gap in the skyline and started crying, and she smashed into his back end. Thank goodness no one was hurt.

There were wider consequences. After the disaster, it became increasingly difficult for Anna to face up to her work as a detective. It was tough on her to leave our kids and to concentrate on the job. The entire experience had driven home to her that life was too short. She wanted to be spending more quality time with me and with our children.

Then, one day in 2011, while she was on her way to the office, she called me. She'd only left the house twenty minutes earlier, perfectly calm, and now she was crying into the phone, almost hysterical. I thought she'd been hurt, but before I could ask a question, she started just shrieking.

"He's dead! He's dead!"

My mind started racing. *Did she run someone down? Kill a pedestrian?*

"What are you talking about? Where are you? Who's dead?"

It took her a few seconds to get it out, but what she was trying to tell me was that she'd just heard on the radio that a team of Navy SEALs had killed Osama bin Laden.

For my wife, the wounds inflicted by 9/11 may never heal. And, as the rest of this story will show, my own personality, and my undercover work, made her life even harder to bear.

7

SMALL(S) BEGINNINGS

By MID-2012, AFTER I HAD COMPLETED a number of UC jobs with the FBI, I received a call from a criminal enterprise investigative unit that was working a string of drug cases. The team wanted me to accompany an associate, "Scott," who had set up a meeting to make a drug buy. Their target was James Heeney, an Elizabeth, New Jersey, drug dealer whose street name was "Jimmy Smalls." This particular dealer had a crew of associates and was known to have ties to the Blood gangs. The investigators suspected that he might be moving weight. Because he had previous firearms and assault convictions, he was a prime target for a federal case. If he was caught with both illegal drugs and a gun, his record of firearms convictions would increase his sentence.

The agreed meeting place was in a steakhouse at a casino in Atlantic City, and the initial deal was for a two-hundred-gram "sampler." I accompanied Scott. We ate dinner and waited—and waited.

Finally, Smalls called us, saying they were on their way, that they'd gotten stuck and were running late. So we waited some more. I ordered some pie for dessert and killed time watching a Yankees game. But it was getting to the point where we had to consider how much longer we would wait. In the underworld, waiting too long can be a red flag—a sign that you are being set up to be robbed. Or killed.

After nearly two hours, and just as we were about to up stakes and leave, Jimmy Smalls showed up, accompanied by two associates. In keeping with the ironies of the street, "Smalls" was an apt nickname. The guy was about 250 pounds, with a thick body, black beard, and an oversized shaved head. One of his companions was a wiry street kid named Frank, and the other a big-boned Hispanic guy who looked like he could handle himself. It was the usual grouping for a drug deal with a first-time customer—the dealer, the sidekick, and the muscle. The three of them strolled in, and Smalls blabbered a token apology. They all sat down at our table, making comments about how hungry they were, and Smalls started talking to Scott about the transaction.

"I got the stuff on me. Where do you want to do it?"

Scott turned to me. "What do you think, Giovanni?"

I glared at Smalls. "What do you mean? You have it on you? You have it on you *here*?"

"Yeah. I got it on me."

It was time for my bad-guy act. "What the hell are you doing with it here in the restaurant? Are you nuts?"

"We don't have to do it here," Smalls replied blithely. "We can go to the bathroom."

His stupidity gave me an opportunity to really lay it on. I pretended to be furious. "What are you?" I hissed. "A fuckin' high school kid, doing deals in the bathroom? Are you crazy? This is a high-end joint! You make us wait here for two hours, and now you show up saying you're hungry? Eat this!" I pushed the remains of my pie across the table. To my surprise, his skinny associate Frank snared the plate and started hoovering up my leftover scraps.

"So, what should we do?" Scott asked.

Putting on my best wiseguy tone, I snapped my fingers at a tiny Italian-looking waitress who passed our table. "Hey, sweetheart, come over here!" She came over, and I said, "You know those to-go bags? We need one here. Go get it."

She fetched one, strode back to our table, and threw it down in front of me. "Here!" She plainly hadn't appreciated my lack of manners.

Feeling ashamed inside, I shot her a smile and softly said, "Thank you, sweetie. I really do appreciate it."

I guess that caught her off guard, because she returned my smile, winked, and said, "You're welcome."

I slid the bag over to Smalls. "Put it in here. Do it under the table."

Smalls and Scott did the deal right there. It went smoothly. I took the bag out to our car, locked it in the trunk, and came back in.

Throughout the transaction, and for the rest of our interaction, I maintained my antagonistic attitude, saying things like "This is stupid, man! Crazy doing this shit like this!" By the time we parted ways, it was pretty clear that Smalls didn't like me much.

But that didn't prevent him from continuing to do business with us. One of the reasons for that, I believe, was because word on the street was that we were Bruno-Scarfo associates—connected to the main Mafia family in the Atlantic City and Philadelphia areas. That was a mistake on our part, but since the damage was done, we figured it might help keep Smalls in line. So during the conversation at the restaurant, Scott played on it a little bit, saying he knew a lot of guys from Philly—neither of us realizing that this little lie would eventually come back to haunt us.

Before we left, Scott asked Smalls when he could get back down to Atlantic City again.

"It's tough for me to come down," he replied, "because of work. I drive a truck."

Scott looked to me. "Giovanni, you're up there in his neck of the woods."

I asked Smalls, "So where are you? Elizabeth?"

"Yeah."

"OK, I can probably work something out. Yeah, let's see."

As I said, that meeting with Jimmy Smalls led to more deals, and his initial dislike of me did diminish over time. The narcotics we bought from him tested out at a high level of purity, and we were hoping to quickly exceed the federal threshold for prosecution and get him off the street permanently.

UC work is based primarily on relationship-building—and greed—and my escalating relationship with Jimmy Smalls gave our team an idea. We had a location full of swag merchandise. It was all material used in the operation as a way of generating credibility on the street by appearing to have ongoing access to "swag" (stolen property). We figured that since we were buying a lot of dope from this guy, maybe we could arrange to pay him with swag and save on spending federal cash. So I gave Smalls a guided tour of the location and put on a little show for him.

He was blown away.

"Wow, look at all this! You guys are selling all this stuff?"

"Yeah."

"Shit, I could really get rid of this for you! We could make some good money!"

"You could sell some of this on the street?"

"Yeah, man! In my neighborhood, I can definitely get rid of this!"

"Well, maybe we could trade. We could trade you for some dope."

"Yeah, yeah. We could work that out!"

Our mistake at the time was that we weren't being careful enough. Our primary aim was to keep the door open with Smalls, so at first we didn't worry about how much swag he took. On our very first transaction, he ended up with about $7,000 worth of stuff, so he owed us big time. The plan was for him to sell the swag in the neighborhood and pay us back with dope. He did sell some of it, and he did make installment payments with dope, but now the lab analyses were revealing that the drugs he was giving us were of very low quality. In one sense, that didn't matter. As long as it comes up positive, coke is coke. A kilo of weak shit is still a kilo, and it is quantity, not quality, that attracts the higher sentence. With that in mind, we let it go.

But soon it was getting harder and harder to collect from him. We had to keep chasing him. We were trying to get this guy up over the kilo mark, but we were getting a hundred grams here, a hundred grams there, and most of it was testing out weak. Then one night I picked up some coke from him that turned out to be total garbage—meaning the package tested negative for *any* controlled dangerous substance.

When that happened, I arranged a meeting with FBI supervisor Dan Conte and Assistant Special Agent in Charge (ASAC) Greg Ehrie.

"Did it have any kind of narcotic in it at all?" Ehrie asked me. "Any kind of poison, any kind of dangerous chemical?"

"No, it was all bullshit. Baby laxative and corn starch."

Hearing that, Ehrie made an inspired call. "If the lab says its garbage, it's garbage. As long as it can't hurt anybody, you can give it back to him. All I need are two separate lab reports stating the same thing and you can put it back on the street."

The lab reports were quickly secured. For me, this was a perfect situation. As a supposed drug criminal, I couldn't let the situation continue unchallenged, and now I could confront Smalls, tell him the drugs he'd been selling us were cut, and shove them back in his face. As the word got around the street, the very fact that I had forced him to take drugs back would provide me with serious credibility.

That is exactly what I did. I called Smalls. "This is garbage! It's all cut! It's all bullshit."

He played dumb. "Really?"

"Are you crazy? I've got a serious problem, and you've created that problem. Now these guys want me to answer for this. The guys I'm giving this stuff to . . . they're serious guys. You've put me in a bad spot, and yourself in a bad spot!"

"Ah, Giovanni, I'm sorry! I'll take it back, you know. I'll take it back. I didn't know it was shit."

"Well, you gotta take this back tonight! And you better make me right by morning!"

"I'm gonna make it right, Giovanni! I promise! I can get you three thousand ecstasy pills . . . but, listen, I'm not around right now." (I thought, *Of course you'd say that.*) "But my boy Mike is. You know, the guy who was with me when I delivered a couple of times?"

"Yeah, yeah."

"You know where the Ribera Club is?"

I knew exactly where the club was, but I said, "I have no fuckin' clue."

"It's a social club. It's in my neighborhood. Just bring it there and—"

I said, "I'm not going into a social club with this!"

"No, no. There's a parking lot right across the street. It's a dead-end street. The Ribera Club's on the left, parking lot's on the right. Mike's pickup truck will be there. Just leave it in the front, under the mat."

I knew all about the Ribera Club. It was a traditional mob hangout. There was one way in and one way out, and patrons always had eyes on the street. Years earlier, I had spent weeks sitting on the place, doing surveillance from the inside of a van. I knew that John Riggi was the boss of the family associated with the club and that these were serious guys. If I got caught dropping off dope near the club, that would be big trouble for me and big trouble for Jimmy Smalls.

It was a bad idea, but I gritted my teeth and drove over there. I yanked open the pickup's passenger door, threw the package under the mat, slammed the door, and stepped back. Immediately, the truck's horn beeped and the doors locked. Obviously, Jimmy's buddy Mike had been waiting and watching up in one of the apartments overlooking the parking lot.

Shortly after that, we met up with Jimmy at an IHOP restaurant in Elizabeth to discuss some cocaine and MDMA deals so he could pay off the balance on his seven-grand debt. He kept blaming his associate Mike for poor sales of the swag. They were high-quality counterfeits from China, so we knew that was bullshit. He should have been able to move them easily on the street. But Smalls was full of excuses.

To test him, I told him he should bring me into the neighborhood to help move the stuff. "If you can't find buyers, bring me around. I'll do my part. I'll do my sales pitch. Just bring me around people."

But he kept deflecting. His constant refrain was "Just give me a bunch of those shoes. Those sneakers! And cigarettes, man! I can sell them in the neighborhood. I can move them, no problem."

"Dude, how can I trust you? I gave you seven Gs worth of shoes and you haven't even paid me for them yet. Instead, you give me shit drugs. Now you want me to give you more stuff? You think I'm a fuckin' *chooch*?"

This dance went on for a few more weeks. It seemed to be taking us nowhere, and our FBI case agents were getting fed up. They didn't want to arrest Smalls right away, because we still hadn't got him up over the threshold. More important, the task force had a longer-term goal and a bigger target in mind: We knew Jimmy's uncle was an old-school Mafia guy named Charles Stango, otherwise known as "Charlie the Hat" or "Charlie Beeps." Stango was a heavy hitter in New Jersey's DeCavalcante crime family—in other words, a real-life *Soprano*—and he was about to be released from prison. It was now well into the spring of 2013, and we'd been dealing with Smalls for several months, half-hoping he'd help us make the jump to somebody in the mob, but it wasn't working out. It was time to change tactics.

Bureau intelligence sources had been telling our agents that Jimmy was getting his drugs from Luigi Oliveri, a known DeCavalcante associate whose street name was "Lui the Dog." It appeared these informants were correct, because Jimmy had been selling most of the swag to Oliveri. We also heard that Oliveri had been asking about us around the neighborhood.

Using street channels, we set up a meeting with him.

8

JEALOUS MISTRESS

MEANWHILE, BACK ON THE HOME FRONT, things were getting tense. My decision to work undercover full time for the Bureau, at this late stage in my career, had proven to be the spark that ignited rising levels of conflict with my wife.

When I'd first discussed the case with Anna, I hadn't gone into details. I just explained that it would be a short-term assignment, and I would be playing a superficial role. At the time, I believed that to be true. But as the operation continued, week after week, month after month, she began to understand how deeply involved I had become. Unlike most spouses, her own police background told her exactly what the implications could be—both for me and for us and the kids. She had done some undercover work herself, although never in long-term or deep cover roles, so when she grasped what I had committed myself to she was livid.

"How could you be such an idiot?" she yelled. "Why would you want to put me and the kids through that? At the end of your career? When most guys are slowing down and getting ready to retire, you're going full speed ahead into something that's going to outlast your time on the job and put us all in danger? What the hell's the matter with you?"

There were also practical problems. Depending on traffic, Anna had a forty-five- to ninety-minute commute to get to her own job, along with an extra thirty-minute side trip to drop off and pick up our son at day care. The nature of her work as a detective meant that she sometimes had to stay late, and it was often logistically more convenient for me to pick up our boy. But as the operation intensified, I became more and more disengaged from the family routines, which placed more and more of the burden on her.

There were, in fact, sound reasons for me to take a step back. Floating around Jersey City, Bayonne, Staten Island, or Elizabeth didn't always fare so well for me. On one occasion, Jimmy Smalls got me mixed up in a drug deal at a location very close to my son's day care facility. Even more worrying was the fact that, as I knew, the address where the deal went down was on law enforcement's target list. If a Narcotics cop had driven by and recognized me sitting in Smalls's car—not knowing I was in an undercover role—there could have been a big problem. Or, worse, if detectives were set up nearby, with eyes on the dealer, and they decided Jimmy Smalls's visit was a good time to take him down, guess who would end up as a witness? Our wider operation could have been destroyed.

I had another close call when I was driving my personal vehicle across the Goethals Bridge from Staten Island to Elizabeth. Traffic was moving at a crawl, and I had my son, who was sound asleep, strapped in a baby seat behind me. Suddenly, Jimmy Smalls started blowing up my phone. Fervently hoping that my boy wouldn't wake up, I answered the call.

"What's up, Jim?"

"Where are you, man? Where are you right now?"

"What's the matter? Whaddya want? What's up?"

"You on the Goethals Bridge?"

Shit.

"What are you talking about, man? Goethals Bridge? No!"

"Are you on the Goethals Bridge? Are you sitting in traffic on the Goethals Bridge?"

"Naw. What are you talking about?"

"Yeah, yeah! What're you—? Are you in a black pickup? I think you just drove by me!"

"What're you talking about? Black pickup truck? I don't have a fuckin' black pickup!" And here I was, sitting in traffic on the Goethals Bridge, behind the wheel of a black pickup.

"I swear to God I just drove by you on the Goethals Bridge! Guy in a black pickup truck. You sure it's not you?"

"No, bro! I'm not on the Goethals Bridge!"

He let it go, but of course he saw me—though I don't know if he saw the baby seat and my son sleeping in the back. That fleeting incident could have ruined everything. I blew him off at the time, and after that, I told Anna I couldn't be doing these pickups and drop-offs, especially since our son's day care was in Bayonne. In that town, if you throw a rock you're going to hit somebody connected to the Mafia.

That incident brought home to both me and my wife just how dangerous it was to be working undercover in the same communities where we resided and commuted. Unsurprisingly, she was furious with me. Not only were my absences burdening her with extra work, on top of commuting to a job that she struggled with emotionally, but also as I got deeper into this case it was more and more difficult to go out anywhere with the family. I had to be extra watchful when we were out in public. If we were going to a restaurant in a mall, we couldn't walk in together. Anna and the kids would have to walk ahead, and I would meet them after they were seated inside the restaurant. But if my little guy had a meltdown while she was walking ahead, I couldn't stop to help her. She was on her own. She could've been pushing a stroller, carrying shopping bags, handling two kids, and feeling overwhelmed—regardless, I couldn't jump to the rescue like moms and dads do. That's because if I didn't spot a mob contact before he spotted me, that contact might see me with my family—a family that wasn't supposed to exist. In an instant, it could be game over. And, when I finally walked into that restaurant to join my family, if I spotted a face from my other life, I'd just have to turn around and walk out.

So this operation was doing exactly what my wife so often warned: "These people you're targeting . . . they're around here, for God's sake! Around us! This is going to ruin us! It's going to destroy our family! And it's as if you don't even care!"

She was right. It *was* slowly destroying our family. We could never just say, "Let's grab the kids and go out to dinner tonight." Everything had to be planned.

My visitations with my two older children also suffered. Because of my fear of being seen with them, we couldn't spend time together like a father and his kids, going out in public or attending sporting events they were involved in.

There was an additional facet to Anna's growing distress about our situation: her innate distrust of the federal government, linked to her father's death while trying to save lives during the 9/11 disaster. The fresh terror injected into her life was not simply that she might also lose her husband—and our children lose their father—but that even if I survived to the end of the investigation, she and I and the kids would end up being cast off and forgotten. The federal government's callous indifference to her mother and her family in the months and years following her father's heroic death had convinced her that when this undercover operation was over, our safety would be treated like a bothersome afterthought.

"Why would you dedicate your time to an organization that just uses people and then throws them away?" she asked. "They don't care about anybody—especially a lowly TFO! They don't give a damn about the family that loves you and wants you to be here and wants to spend time with you. Why are you putting this burden on us, giving your life over to a government that you've already seen screw over your wife's family and so many others?"

At the time, in the thick of the operation, my obsession with the case and my selfishness blinded me to the wisdom of her words. I shrugged it off, telling myself, *Oh, she's just angry about the loss of her father.*

The fact is, I had no good answer. I was determined to continue, and as I readily admit today, too often I simply closed my ears to Anna's justified complaints and astute warnings. I knew damn well it was a bad choice to be running this long-term operation right in our own backyard. But to me, then, covert work was my passion. It was my jealous mistress.

Looking back, and being honest, I have to admit that this mistress was an addiction—an addiction I just wasn't ready to kick, even for my own family. I was always a bit of a bastard, and that helped me to do the job, but the job itself was turning me into an even worse bastard.

I was self-aware enough to eventually recognize that, and in moments of honesty, looking in the mirror, I could see exactly what I was and what I had become.

So whenever I returned home, I went through a little ritual. I parked in the driveway, removed my "Giovanni ring," as I called it, and dropped it in a cup holder. It was a jeweled pinkie ring that I wore as a prop during my undercover life. Back at the beginning of the operation, the FBI had let me select it. Within the mob, such a ring was a symbol of respect. It was just like the ones worn by the old-style Italian mob bosses, and wearing it mentally positioned me where I needed to be as an up-and-comer—as a younger guy who was showing respect for the old ways.

But that ring was symbolic in another way. By removing it before entering the house, I was trying to take a necessary mental step toward reinhabiting my real life, trying to become my *real* self again. After the removal, for a few minutes I talked myself out of being Giovanni Gatto and back into being Anna's husband and the father of our children. The point of the exercise was to train myself to leave my undercover personality out there in the driveway. Out there in the car.

But as time passed, the more I tried to leave that Gatto bastard out in the car, the more I failed. Worse than that, I got to a point where I didn't even care that I failed. Those were my days of shame, when I couldn't deal with my own family life because my work was more important, when every move I made had the potential of putting Anna and the kids in danger.

9

LUI THE DOG

WORD MUST HAVE GOTTEN OUT in the neighborhood about "this Giovanni Gatto guy with all the swag," because a few days before our agreed meeting with Luigi Oliveri, Jimmy Smalls called me in a panic. Somehow he must have discovered what we were planning.

Right away, he tried to convince me to stay away from Lui the Dog: "The guy's no good, Giovanni. He'll never make it into the books, he'll never be anybody. He wants to get made in the mob, but he's never gonna be anybody."

"How the hell would you know all this?"

"My Uncle Charlie."

"Who's he?"

"Uncle Charlie? He's Charlie Stango."

"Never heard of him."

"Oh, my God! My Uncle Charlie's, you know, he's a made guy! He's a soldier. He's killed people. He's going be a captain."

"Well, that's good for you. He's your uncle. Nice. But what does that mean for us?"

"Well, he's locked up right now. He's getting out soon. He's due to move back to New Jersey to finish his parole. He says he'll be back in the area sometime next month."

"Sounds good, but you haven't answered my question."

"He can help us, Giovanni! Believe me, he can!"

When I told the case agents about the call, they started thinking that maybe Jimmy was worth the effort after all. Maybe he could give us access to his uncle. "But keep the meeting with Luigi," they instructed. "We need him as a fallback."

Early in June, accompanied by an associate named Tommy, I met Luigi Oliveri outside the Woodbridge Center, a shopping mall near Elizabeth, New Jersey. Oliveri had originally suggested that we meet him at the Ribera Club, but I nixed the idea. I already knew that Jimmy Smalls had connections with the club, and since he didn't know for sure that we were meeting with Luigi, I didn't want to take a chance on him walking in at the wrong moment.

We met up in the mall's parking lot, in front of Dick's Sporting Goods. And who was standing there, right next to Luigi? Mike—the same guy Jimmy Smalls had been blaming for the bad dope and the disappointing swag sales. It was all so tangled and interwoven, and so stupid. It was obvious they must have been talking to each other.

As we walked toward him, Luigi was visibly wary and on edge. During the initial conversation, he kept his eyes locked on me. He didn't seem too concerned about Tommy, just about me. I don't know what it was—maybe the way I was dressed. I was clean-cut, with nice shoes, button-down shirt, typical slick Italian wear. The Dog, on the other hand, was aptly named. He looked like a soup sandwich—overweight, droopy eyelids, and sloppily dressed in a wrinkled baby-blue shirt, faded jeans, and a scruffy cloth cap that, as I would later discover, he hardly ever took off.

To make things easier for the surveillance team, I said, "Listen, I'm going inside to get a coffee. Why don't you come?" Just the suggestion that he follow along seemed to ruffle his feathers. It was as if I was taking charge and he didn't like it. But he came with us. Tommy took his coffee and he and Mike wandered out into the mall, leaving Luigi and me to ourselves.

As soon as we sat down, he started asking about the swag. "What's your stuff?" he asked. "What do you have? You got sneakers too?"

"And shirts, and shoes, and wallets, and purses. And cigarettes. All kinds."

"Is it all bootleg shit?"

"For the most part, but the cigarettes are real. All legit."

"Yeah? I've got a pretty good network, Giovanni. Guys call me. You should sell it to me in bulk. All the stuff you gave that kid Jimmy . . . that came to me."

"The whole seven grand's worth?"

"Yeah. He brought all of it to my grandmother's house in Elizabeth."

"You mean that garage? At the end of the dead-end street?"

"Wait! *You guys* brought it there?" He looked shocked. "He didn't bring it there?"

"Yeah, we backed up the truck. Put it in the garage."

"Fuck! That's my grandmother's house!"

So, right out of the gate, he was pissed off at Jimmy for bringing outsiders to his grandmother's house and dropping off stolen goods on the property.

I nudged the subject toward our pet peeve. "Listen, he still hasn't paid me the balance."

"What do you mean?"

"He owes me a lot of money. He's trying to pay it off with dope, but he's got a long way to go."

"Well, I was going to ask for more stuff."

"I'd be happy to do business with you, but nobody's getting any more until I get my money. Nobody's getting nothing."

"Don't let him slide on it."

"I don't plan to, but I don't want any problems with the kid. He told me who his uncle is. His Uncle Charlie."

"What about him?"

"He told me the uncle's hooked up. Told me he's a soldier. I think he said . . . 'a captain.'"

"What? He didn't . . . He told you that?"

"Yeah, so I do not want any fuckin' problems. I don't want this uncle stepping up and squashing me like a bug."

"Listen, you shouldn't let him slide just on who his uncle is. And he's not a captain. He's real good guy, a serious guy . . . but he's a hot-head—short tempered. Known him my whole life." He stopped there, probably thinking he was saying too much.

He switched over to suggesting a way to approach Jimmy about what he still owed. "Here's what you do. Tell him you asked some guys you know—guys in another family. And they talked to some DeCav guys who told you to see Lui the Dog from Fourth Avenue. You watch his reaction when you say that to him. See if he don't shit his pants."

"Who the fuck is Lui the Dog?"

"Me."

"So, I just say that to him? 'Lui the Dog?'"

"Yeah . . . just say your people reached out to the DeCavs, and they put you in touch with me, and then I came and had a sit-down with you. That's the way you deal with Jimmy—scare the shit outta him."

I understood exactly what he was saying. This is how the Mafia operates—manipulation and playing on fear has always been one of the keys to its survival. I also realized that this move might help put out any potential fires caused by me having to deal with Jimmy and Luigi at the same time.

"OK," I said. "I might try that."

With that settled, he started probing me a little. "So, where are you from?"

"South Jersey. I just moved back up this way. What's that got to do with—?"

"No, I mean, where are your people from?"

"My father's family is originally from Calabria."

"Oh, I'm from Sicily, so we're practically related."

I shrugged my shoulders. "Yeah, but I'm not all Italian. I got a little bit of Irish in me on my mom's side."

By this point, Luigi was looking a lot more relaxed than when we'd first met. "All right," he said. "I'm gonna get back to you. We'll talk."

As we parted, I said, "Ciao." I wasn't trying to imply that I was fluent in Italian, but in that world, it's sometimes the casual little touches that count.

"OK, ciao."

When I returned to the task force office, I explained how Luigi might be able to help us with getting Jimmy Smalls to pay off his debt. After getting the go-ahead, I called Jimmy and parroted what Luigi had suggested—that my people had reached out to the DeCavs, and they'd set up a meeting with Luigi Oliveri. As Luigi had predicted, Jimmy got really nervous. "No, no, Giovanni! I'm gonna make it right! Gonna make it right! Don't tell Lui!"

A couple of weeks later, Luigi called me. "Listen, I'm having this thing in my neighborhood, in Peterstown. It's the section of Elizabeth where we live. It's an old-school Italian feast. You should come."

I said, "Yeah, maybe I will."

On the heels of this, Jimmy Smalls called to tell me he had three thousand ecstasy pills, and he wanted to pass them over to clear part of his debt. When he said I could pick up the pills from him at the Italian feast in Peterstown, I immediately agreed.

On the appointed day, I hooked up with Jimmy at an apartment just outside the venue of the feast. We did the ecstasy deal there, and after checking the pill count and heat-sealing them in bags, we were done.

Then Jimmy said, "C'mon, take a walk with me. We'll go through the feast."

So here I was, escorted into the heart of the neighborhood by well-known local Jimmy Smalls. A band was playing Italian music, people were dancing in the street, and older men and women were sitting on couches that had been carried out from their homes. The atmosphere was completely familiar—a neighborhood closeness that reminded me of my childhood years in Bayonne. But that was as far as it went, because in this community, I was a foreigner.

As we strolled along, heads turned and wary eyes followed our progress. Uncannily, everyone seemed to be hyperaware of us. I guessed these people had been hearing about Jimmy flogging bootlegged shoes, purses, and cigarettes, and now here he comes with this *gabone*.

Eventually, I spied Luigi at the little sausage stand he'd told me he'd be running. There he was, surrounded by his crew, cooking and talking and scanning faces. As soon as he saw me, our eyes locked. His expression said, "I see ya. I see ya there with Jimmy." We exchanged smirks, and I rolled my eyes toward Smalls, who at that moment was looking the other way. Luigi nodded his head, as if to say, *Yeah. He's a fuckin' jerk.*

We did our little walk-through, and the whole time, Luigi's crew was watching. I could see Luigi talking to them, and I imagined he was saying, *That's the guy. See Jimmy's guy over there? He's gonna be my guy.*

Near the center of activity was a huge statue of the Mother Mary. In front of it was a plastic swimming pool. You were supposed to throw in money—purportedly money for the church. The reality, I suspected, was that none of the money would go to the church—it would all go to the DeCav family. A few old men and women were sitting next to the pool, making sure nobody stole any of the contributions. Without skipping a beat, I reached into my pocket and threw in a fifty.

It looked good. It looked the part.

We continued on, checking out some of the shops and stalls, and palming through some of the junk people were selling. I bought a Lamborghini T-shirt from a stall directly across from Luigi's tent. I knew the shirt was *fugazy*—pure fake—but the point was to be seen interacting. I yukked it up a bit with the vendor, deliberately being a bit loud, making sure some of the watchers could hear, doing a bit of a dance for the targets and keeping it real.

Strangely, when I mentioned I was hungry, Jimmy led me over to Luigi's stand. When he said, "Great food, here, Giovanni! Owner's a friend of mine," it was all I could do not to burst out laughing. I bought a sausage sandwich from one of Lui's guys—sausage, peppers, and onions— all the while exchanging mocking glances with Luigi when Jimmy wasn't paying attention. When I sat down to eat, Jimmy stood there next to me, his chest all puffed out, in a laughable attempt to show me off. In response, Luigi sent one of his guys over to fuck with Jimmy's head while I was sitting there. The whole pantomime was like a dimwitted pissing match, and I had a good laugh about it later with my case agent.

While I was driving, I texted Luigi: "Thanks for today. It all worked out. Sorry we couldn't have coffee."

He shot me a reply: "OK. You got it."

He and I talked on the phone later. I told him I had followed his advice about scaring the shit out of Jimmy and it had worked, because he'd just done us a deal that cleared off a chunk of his debt. After he and I agreed on a meeting about a swag deal, Luigi said, "Thanks for doing what you did today. It was good. If we see each other again on the street, we don't know each other. Play it dumb."

I agreed.

From then on, whenever Tommy and I did a deal with Smalls, he would say, "Don't tell Luigi," and whenever we sold some swag to Luigi, he would say, "Don't tell Jimmy."

Despite the moments of private humor, it had been a tense few hours. My foray into Peterstown and the neighborhood feast, under the undisguised scrutiny of suspicious locals, had been utterly draining. It had required all of the skills drummed into me by my course instructors—and all of the habits of mind and behavior that I had picked up as a kid on the streets—to project just the right persona during those hours.

That evening, when I finally got home to my real family, I was more than ready to let it all go—to shed my Giovanni ring, leave that Gatto character in the car, go into the house, enjoy my wife and children, watch TV, and just decompress.

It was not to be. Unknown to me, the actor James Gandolfini—internationally known and admired for his role as Tony Soprano—had died the day before. Almost every TV channel was paying tribute to the man, with HBO featuring key Tony Soprano moments from *The Sopranos* TV series. The HBO retrospective was simply titled *Our Friend*.

Unnervingly, some of the clips they showed had been filmed in the same Peterstown neighborhood I had just left. And many of them reminded me of the true nature of the world I now inhabited: a world without honor, whose inhabitants could easily refer to me as "our friend" today and, without a moment's thought, put a bullet in my head tomorrow.

The world had lost James Gandolfini—an actor I greatly admired—but Tony Soprano had played out his role on the solid footing of a film set. Giovanni Gatto was playing out his on the tightrope of grim reality.

There would be no decompression for me that night, nor for many nights to come.

Over the following weeks, I continued dealing with Luigi, selling him cases of cigarettes, shoes, and clothing, and it was going well. This guy was always good with his money. Every time I showed up, he would pull out a wad of cash and peel off the bills.

A few times I made deliveries down at his social club in Elizabeth. Unlike the Ribera Club, which was situated two blocks away, this club had no apparent name—it was just a former storefront with horizontal blinds, tinted windows, poker tables, and *Godfather* and *Sopranos* posters covering the walls. This was Luigi's favorite spot, and he had a regular card game going on there two or three nights a week. By now I was comfortable enough with meeting him there.

Meanwhile, the FBI team began hearing (through intelligence sources, and from cops on the street) that people in the key neighborhoods in Elizabeth, including Peterstown, were getting wind that the neighborhoods were being looked at, that law enforcement was targeting the DeCavs. The agents didn't know where the warning was coming from, but it naturally caused concern that there might be a leak inside law enforcement—and, therefore, concern for my safety.

At around the same time, Luigi set up a deal with me and asked if I would come to his club to deliver some North Face jackets, shoes, and cigarettes. While I was there, Luigi offered to make me a cup of espresso.

After I sat down, he said, "You know, our people are saying cops are trying to take a shot at us around here."

"And?"

"And, you're new."

"So, what are you getting at?"

"I'm just saying, you know, it's weird that you come around now, and next thing, there's buzz on the street that cops are trying to set us up."

"Spit it out. What are you saying? You want to ask me something, Lou?"

"Well, how long you know Jimmy?"

I deliberately raised my voice. "That's got nothing to fucking do with it! Listen, I've been doing business with you for how long now? And, I'm well into Jimmy, and he's still walking the streets!"

He backed off. "Yeah, well, I'm just telling you."

So I managed to shrug it off and it went away—that time. But the flame of suspicion never went out. It was always there, burning low.

10

MAKING THE JUMP: GAMBINOS

As JIMMY HAD TOLD ME, when his uncle Charlie Stango was to be released from prison, he would be returning to New Jersey. And, as our task force learned through surveillance and from well-placed informants, as soon as Stango arrived home, he was made up to capo. From that moment on, he was officially a captain in the DeCavalcante crime family.

The ceremony itself took place at a Holiday Inn. Unknown to the family, it was surveilled by the FBI. This development, and the fact that I was already in tight with both Stango's nephew and DeCav associate Luigi Oliveri, prompted our case agents to turn the operational spotlight on Stango himself. Previous investigations, and FBI intelligence, had revealed that two of Stango's closest friends were high-level members of the Gambino crime family, the Gambinos effectively being the DeCavalcante's parent organization. One of these figures was Danny "Gooms" Bertelli, a man known to have had past dealings with Jimmy Smalls. Another was Nino Molinelli, a crew boss who had once worked for John Gotti. Both men had "juice" and were well-respected by all the families.

The problem we faced was how to engineer an "accidental" encounter that would help us make the jump to Charlie Stango.

As it happened, we knew that Bertelli and Molinelli frequented a particular restaurant—Anthony's Coal Fired Pizza, in Clifton, New Jersey. The pair met there for lunch almost every Friday. It was a long shot, but if I could arrange for Jimmy to meet me at the same restaurant when the Gambino guys were there, I might be able to make something happen.

I set up a Friday lunch meeting with Smalls at Anthony's Coal Fired Pizza, and I brought Tommy along with me. When Jimmy showed up, he was accompanied by an associate we hadn't met before. I found out later the guy was a Crips street gang member who had recently been released from jail. He was working on the truck with Jimmy, doing deliveries, and because it was the middle of a workday, both of them were sweaty and covered in grime.

The professed reason for our meeting was to do a quick deal for a few hundred grams of MDMA. Tommy and I had arrived early, and I made sure we were sitting near the Gambino guys' regular table. I did that, first, to be sure that we were within reasonable proximity to the mobsters and, second, because of the unique feature of Jimmy Smalls's anatomy—his oversized head. Actually, it's such an abnormally—indeed, unbelievably—large head that the guy is almost impossible not to notice. (If that were an indicator of a high IQ, Jimmy could have been the next Einstein. But apparently cranium size is not a factor.)

Sure as anything, partway through lunch, Bertelli left his table, heading for the bathroom. As he passed our group, he did an almost cartoonish double take.

"Jimmy Smalls?"

"Huh? Oh, hi, Danny! Yeah, how're you doin'? I thought that was you."

Bertelli scanned our table. "What are you doing?"

"Nothing, nothing." Jimmy jumped up and gave Bertelli the kiss. The mobster immediately pulled him off to one side. They talked for a couple of minutes and then came back. Jimmy introduced us, and added, "Yeah, I'm doing cigarettes with these guys, and a few other things, so maybe . . ."

Bertelli evaluated us through narrowed eyes. "Yeah . . . maybe I'll be in touch. Give me a number where I can reach you."

After he left, Jimmy blurted, "Wow, this is crazy. That guy—I think that just opened a big door for us!"

"How do you figure?"

"He's one of my uncle's guys, a real close associate. He's with the Gambinos, and the two other guys sitting at the table, they're made guys." He was referring to Nino Molinelli and a third man at Bertelli's table, a Scarfo associate known as "Nicky the Whip."

I just said, "All right. If you say so."

For a few weeks, we heard nothing. Then I got a call from Jimmy.

"You know that Gambino guy we talked to—Danny? He wants to see us. He might want to do some business."

I figured it was time to give Jimmy a little blast of cold air to remind him where he stood. "He wants to see 'us?' Who the fuck is 'us?' Number one, you still owe me money, Jimmy! You're close. You're getting there, but you still owe me a couple of grand. Remember that!"

We met Bertelli for coffee at the Union Plaza Diner in Union, New Jersey—an old-time gangster hangout. No sooner had we sat down when Bertelli started bombarding me with questions. "So what have you been up to? Who do you hang out with? Where are you from?"

I told him I was from South Jersey.

"Yeah? Got some things confused here." His eyes bored into me. "Heard you were from Philly."

So there it was again: the Bruno-Scarfo story coming back to bite me in the ass. Luigi had already asked me the same question.

Bertelli pressed. "So, you're not with anybody?"

"Not with anybody. I don't know why that keeps coming up."

"All right. So, what are you guys into? Jimmy says cigarettes? Where do you get cigarettes?"

"I get 'em. That's all you really need to know."

That might sound insolent, but I knew he would like that response. Yes, I had a cover story all prepared—about a string of corrupt warehouse guys who kept me supplied. If I'm hard-pressed and need to deliver, then yes, I'll tell the story. The inexperienced officer would answer, "Yeah, I have cigarettes! And this is how I get them, and this is where I get them, and I have buyers all over, and I sell them to this guy and that guy, and . . . yada, yada, yada." It's the worst thing to do. The officer would look like a big mouth, and big mouths can't be trusted.

Bertelli said, "OK, give me some samples and we'll see what we can do. I know a guy who might want some. I might be able to move some of the cigarettes for you. But you gotta give me a good number, a good price."

So I gave him a price, and he took some samples and went off.

Much later, I discovered that Charlie Stango himself was the hidden hand behind that pivotal meeting with Bertelli. Unknown to me at the time, the FBI had a reliable informant inside the Ribera Club, and he was supplying intelligence on the DeCavalcante family. This confidential source happened to overhear a conversation between Charlie Stango and Danny Bertelli, the gist of which was the following:

> BERTELLI: "I saw your nephew with a couple of guys the other day."
>
> STANGO: "You saw Jimmy?"
>
> BERTELLI: "Yeah. He was with a couple of guys. They're into some stuff—swag, cigarettes."
>
> STANGO: "What did they look like?"
>
> BERTELLI: "Capable. Put together. They look like they shouldn't be hanging out with your nephew!"
>
> STANGO: "Oh yeah? Look into them for me, will you? See what's going on."

11

CREEPING SUSPICIONS

I WAS STILL DEALING WITH LUIGI OLIVERI, and not long after our session with Danny Bertelli, I met up with the Dog to deliver more cases of cigarettes. But this time, he wasn't there just to do a deal.

We were standing in a mall parking lot, and he started right in, asking the same old question. "So, who are you with, Giovanni? Like, you're not with anybody?"

"This again? I told you. I'm not with anybody."

"Listen, like . . . me—I'm with the DeCavalcante family." That's what he said—he put it right out there. "So, are you represented by anybody?"

"No. I'm not represented by anybody."

"See, that's what bothers me, Giovanni. You got to be close to my age, right? Like in your forties."

"Yeah."

"So, where have you been for forty-some years?"

"Why does this come up now? Why you keep bringing this up?"

"Because it just bothers me."

I knew I'd better deal with this head on. And I had an idea how.

"Listen, Lou," I said. "I'm not with anybody, and nobody represents me. But if I need somebody, that's different. If I'm going to war with somebody, yeah, I got a fuckin' army I can call." My sleeves were rolled up, so I tapped the lone-wolf tattoo on my forearm. "Growing up, all my family and friends were outlaw bikers. I got this tattoo because I answer for myself and I take care of things myself if I can."

"Ah . . . OK." I could see the lightbulb go on.

"Yeah. So if that's what you're asking me, that's who I am. But if you and me ever had a problem—I'm not saying we will—but, you know, if I ever had to go to war, I got people I can call."

"Oh, OK. All right, all right."

Later that same day, we discovered why Luigi had been pressing those buttons. The investigators received information that Charlie Stango had called Oliveri and told him that his girlfriend—Charlie's girlfriend, a woman named Patricia "Patty" Malone—had found out that Jimmy Smalls had been selling drugs to undercover cops for the past year.

In my mind, that didn't necessarily refer to me. It could have been operatives from any law enforcement agency, because Smalls was dealing drugs to any customer he could find. But it was a very disturbing development, and our case agents were becoming increasingly worried about a law enforcement leak.

But who? And how?

The next day, when I called Luigi, he told me he would call back later and said to answer my phone when it rang. That meant he was switching phones. He did call me later, and we both changed and exchanged numbers. But when I texted him at the new number, he answered by telling me he was "getting new digits." In other words, he was changing phones again. After that, he went completely dark, and I lost all contact with him.

In the meantime, while the FBI was still trying to figure out where the leak was coming from, both Jimmy Smalls and Danny Bertelli broke off contact with me as well. Days turned into weeks, and I heard nothing from my primary customers. Meanwhile, the team got word that Charlie Stango had arranged to transfer his parole to Nevada. Apparently, he wanted to go into business in some club out there. Just when it had looked like I might make contact with Charlie Stango, he was leaving.

The case agents asked me to set up a meeting with Luigi and test the waters about the source of the leak. But just as I was trying to make that happen, the entire undercover operation expired. A decision to continue and renew an operation can sometimes be burdensome.

The timing could not have been worse. Administrative rules were creating headaches just when I was in mid-jump to Charlie Stango, and Stango was about to move out west. With the FBI chasing a law enforcement leak about the operation and our targets possibly starting to wonder if I was a cop, I realized I needed to do some serious damage control. But because of FBI policy, my hands were tied. I couldn't call. I couldn't text. I couldn't even send a carrier pigeon. It was typical "Bureau-cratic" bullshit, as some agents referred to it. So I recruited a low-level associate to put the word on the street that I had to go away for a while, that I had some issue to clear up, that I'd gone out of state to deal with it.

Not long after this, Jimmy started burning up my phone, leaving voicemails. He'd finally discovered that Luigi and I had been doing business, and that Luigi was putting some of my swag on the street. Jimmy was calling because he was pissed off, figuring he was being cut out of the action. I had no option but to ignore his calls until, at last, our case agents got the green light to continue the operation. I was back in the game.

During the long wait, Luigi had also begun calling again. Receiving no answer, he had started asking around on the street, trying to find out where I was. Having in mind Jimmy Smalls's hysterical voicemails complaining about me dealing directly with Luigi, I decided to keep it real and turn things around on these guys. So I created a new story. I put it on the street that, if anybody asked where I was, "You can say I'm pissed off with these guys because they can't shoot straight. They can't get their shit together. Maybe if they get their shit together, I'll come back around."

12

FIRST CONTACT

EVEN THOUGH THE OPERATION WAS BACK UP AND RUNNING, I let the calls from Jimmy and Luigi go to voicemail a few more times before I responded. Although I did finally reconnect with them, my primary target was still the elusive Charlie Stango. Learning from Jimmy that his uncle was still in New Jersey, I scored some ringside seats to a UFC fight in Newark. My thinking was that if I told Jimmy I had the tickets, his uncle might want to come along. That didn't work out because nobody was available.

As I was trying to figure out some other way to manipulate either Jimmy, Luigi, or Danny Bertelli into getting me a meeting with Capo Stango, the problem solved itself. Unknown to me, Danny Bertelli had already recommended to Stango that the two of us should meet.

On January 29, I was invited back to the Union Plaza Diner. When I walked through the front door, Smalls and Bertelli and Stango were already there. Jimmy waved me over. I said hello to everyone, and introduced myself to Charlie Stango. He greeted me very cordially and told me to take the seat next to him.

During the early part of the conversation, Stango didn't say much. He just locked on to me and stared. It was a half-intimidating sort of stare that said, *I'm a serious guy, kid. Pay close attention.* He was almost the stereotype of all those wiseguys you ever saw in a movie. He was the older version of them: short, narrow shoulders, pants pulled up, with his arms turned in on the table. He just sat there, listening to every word I said and watching every gesture I made. I could tell he was the real deal. The fact that he was so eerily quiet made him seem almost scary. He was making it clear that I was no threat to him—that *he* was the threat.

When he finally spoke, he got straight to the point: "My nephew here—he says you've been doing a lot of business with him."

"Yeah, we've been doing some good business." I paused for effect. "We've had our bumps in the road, and I didn't throw him under the bus yet." I looked straight at Jimmy, who was sitting across the table from me. "It hasn't been easy, but we're getting there."

Charlie knew what I was saying, and I could tell that he liked it. I wasn't telling him his nephew's a douche bag, or crying about how much money the kid owed me. I was just saying that we're working it out.

Charlie's eyes cut to his nephew, his expression saying, *You're a fuckin' idiot.* He continued: "Jimmy says you've been doing business a long time—almost, what, a year? Whatever it is. And Danny here, he's been watching you. Says you've got some cigarettes and some other stuff, and you're doing some things."

"Yeah."

"Nobody's got anything bad to say about you, and the people that know you say good things, so seems like you're OK. I just wanted to meet you. I wanted to put eyes on you. I'm moving to Las Vegas. Maybe you guys are gonna keep doing what you're doing. You're doing things with Danny, and you're doing things with my nephew here. I could allow it to go on."

I said, "That would be great. I think we can make some money together."

"All right. Well, like I said. Keep doing what you're doing, and we'll go from there. Whatever you do, though, whatever you're gonna do on the street, you do it because I said you could. Understand?"

"I understand. Me and Jimmy, we'll be OK."

Stango's next comment was aimed primarily at his nephew. "I want no fuckin' problems from you guys. You understand, Jimmy? You understand what I'm saying to you right now?"

"Yeah. Yeah, I do, Uncle." Jimmy looked a bit shamefaced—and a bit afraid.

"Listen to me. I got Danny Gooms here as a witness. I'm telling you right now: you're my nephew, so I'm putting you on record with me."

When Stango said that, Jimmy's head came up. He looked stunned. Had he finally crossed the line of acceptance with his uncle? I could almost hear his exuberant thoughts: *Maybe, finally, Uncle Charlie actually believes I can do something good!*

My immediate thought was that there was a hidden agenda here. My guess was that Stango went on record for the kid in front of Danny Bertelli as a way of keeping his nephew from getting clipped. He went on record because he knew that if Jimmy Smalls did something stupid when he was doing deals with Danny, or screwed up anything that affected Danny's cut, the Gambinos wouldn't hesitate to kill him. By taking that step in front of Danny, he was signaling, *This kid is with me.*

But I also sensed that he was saying something more. He meant, *Listen. This kid Giovanni here—do what you want with him. But this is my nephew, Gooms. He's on record with me. Don't kill him. Call me.*

Earlier in the conversation, Charlie had mentioned that he was leaving for Las Vegas that same day. As we wrapped up the meeting, he said, "I'll touch base with you guys soon. I'm moving to Vegas. My parole officer granted me approval to move there, and that's what's going to happen. Good luck. I gotta go . . . get my flight."

And that was that. Everyone stood up, and Charlie said, "Giovanni, a pleasure to meet you. Maybe we'll talk. We'll see."

13

OPERATION
CHARLIE HORSE

On February 6, 2014, I received word from Jimmy Smalls that his uncle wanted to talk to me. It was a conversation that was destined to change everything, because it signaled that I had made the jump to a DeCavalcante family legend—Charlie Stango was an old-time gangster with strong ties to the Gambinos and, as I would later learn, good connections to the Lucchese, Genovese, and Colombo families. This meant our FBI case would have to make a jump as well. What had begun as a drug investigation targeting Jimmy Smalls and his street gang associates now became a full-blown LCN investigation. That meant removing the case from the current task force and handing it over to one of the Bureau's Italian Organized Crime units.

There was a bit of an internal fight over that before the transition happened, including a dispute over who was going to be the new primary case agent. The operation was eventually transferred to the traditional LCN squad at the FBI office in Newark. The new case agent was a young guy named Ray. At first, I was a bit worried about the transfer, but when I learned that Ray would be our case agent, my concerns evaporated. We'd already met, and I knew his goals would mesh perfectly with my own. Right from the start, he and I agreed that, come hell or high water, we were going headfirst into the DeCavalcante family.*

The Bureau, in a stroke of weird logic, designated the transformed investigation "Operation Charlie Horse."

———————

The DeCavalcante family was, and is, based in both New Jersey and New York. The family's head office, if it could be called that, was in New York. However, compared to the notorious Five Families of New York Mafia lore, the current DeCavs had been described as the Gambinos' "redheaded stepchild." They had always aspired to be one of the A-listers, but in recent decades, they couldn't get out of their own way. They were mostly hired to do enforcement. The Gambinos referred to them as "the farmers," or "the farm team," because they farmed out a lot of their murders to DeCavalcante soldiers. In mob parlance, they "flew their flag" under the Gambinos.

For me, that made this operation even more dangerous. Knowing the DeCavs were prone to violence, hungry for notoriety, and constantly seeking to prove themselves to the other families meant I would need to be on perpetual high alert.

As unlikely as this may sound, the DeCavalcantes were one of the first Italian American crime families. They have been around for almost a century and, for most of that time, were the dominant La Cosa Nostra family in northern New Jersey. Some of the members I eventually met, men like Charlie "Big Ears" Majuri, and Luca "Milk" Vitale, were the sons and grandsons of mobsters who had been involved in the creation of the LCN Commission back in the 1930s. That organization, the brainchild of Charles "Lucky" Luciano, was the equivalent of a national board of directors for all the mob families. Its creation was agreed at a secret meeting in Chicago in 1931, where Luciano, Al Capone, and more than twenty other Mafia bosses from across the continent met to end interfamily wars and establish lasting criminal prosperity. Sam

———————

* Ray turned out to be my most reliable lifeline throughout the rest of the investigation, and we remain good friends to this day.

"the Plumber" DeCavalcante was the original family boss. He had run the organization efficiently and was well respected. But after him, it had been mostly downhill. One of his successors, an acting boss named John D'Amato, turned out to be bisexual. That news proved too much for the other family members, and they had him killed. (Sound familiar, *Sopranos* fans?)

During my UC operation, the DeCavalcante boss was John "the Eagle" Riggi, a no-nonsense guy and, by mob standards, an effective manager who had gained the respect of all five families. He ran the organization with an iron fist and had no problem ordering a hit, or even killing people himself. Everyone in the family feared him and respected him.*

Along with the traditional loan sharking and illegal gambling, Riggi controlled a lot of union activity in the Newark/Elizabeth area—construction work, transportation work, and major contracts on bridges and highways. For several years he ran the organization from prison. He was released in November 2012, shortly after my first contact with Jimmy Smalls, and would die, age ninety, only a few months after our operation ended.

The family's home base in New Jersey was the Ribera Club, in Elizabeth.

As for Charlie Stango, in the old days he had been an up-and-comer in the family. He was a solid street guy from Elizabeth, born and raised in "the neighborhood." In his younger days, he ran around with a guy named Ray Tango. If something needed to be dealt with, they had no problem doing the job, even killing someone. They'd carry out any order. Whatever the family wanted, this pair would do it. In the 1970s and '80s, Charlie had a serious drug problem, to the point where he was using a lot of cocaine. He would get high and just beat or kill people. I guess that's what made it easier for him to do it.

In 1980, Charlie Stango, Ray Tango, and a third associate named Lou Pasquarosa murdered a man named Billy Mann. They lured him

---

* Some believe that the Tony Soprano character was modeled after John Riggi and that the DeCavalcante family was the inspiration for *The Sopranos* TV series. The creator of that series has denied this.

to a meeting at the Newark Airport Sheraton, drove him around to the back of the hotel, and shot him multiple times. Mann stumbled out of the car and tried to crawl away, but they opened up on him and finished him off. Unfortunately for them, during the fusillade inside the car Pasquarosa accidentally took a bullet in the shoulder. He was arrested at a hospital, eventually flipped on Stango and Tango, and told the police officers where they could find the car.

In November 1981, Charlie was convicted of Mann's murder and for conspiring to kill Pasquarosa, who had agreed to testify against him. He received a long sentence, serving both federal time and state time. After I got to know him, he would often bitch about serving two terms for the same crime, but that wasn't true. One was for Mann's murder, and one was for conspiracy to murder the cooperating witness.

But now Charlie Stango was out on federal probation and itching to get back in the action.

14

PLANTING THE FLAG

WHEN JIMMY TOLD ME HIS UNCLE WANTED TO TALK, he gave me a contact number. I made the call, and Charlie answered right away. He said he would call me back from a different number.*

As promised, a few minutes later he called me back. "You should have this number," he said. "Only a couple of my goombahs have it. And now you have it. You understand what I'm saying to you?"

"Yeah. You're telling me if I need to call you, use this number."

"No. What I'm telling you is the only people that have this number are my goombahs and now you have it. So listen. You're gonna fly my flag." Those were his exact words: "*You're gonna fly my flag.*"

At that moment, I think my heart stopped, because I understood what that meant.

"You get me?"

"Yeah, I get you, Charlie."

"If I need you, I'm going to call you, so make sure you answer."

"OK."

"If you don't, I'm gonna call Jimmy to track you down. But don't make me come chasing after you. You have to be there now, you understand?"

---

* As time went on, Charlie would always call me on one number and tell me to call him back on another number. There was a system to it. If I called him on his cell phone, I would just say, "Hey, it's me," and he'd say, "Call me on the left," meaning, *Hang up and call me on my burner phone so we can talk business.*

"Yeah. I understand."

"All right. So this is how it's gonna go: You're gonna make some money, but you're under my flag. You understand what that means? You're flying under my flag, which means you're with me now."

"Yes, I get it."

"All right. Let's see how it goes from here."

That officially made me an associate of Charlie Stango—that is, an associate *within* the DeCavalcante crime family, although not yet an associate *of* the family. He didn't go on record for me with the Administration; that would be a bigger step. But he had put me down as flying his flag, which meant I'd be reporting to him. He didn't say anything more about money, but I knew that subject would be raised again soon.

With that one phone call, I was in. The FBI team was very, very pleased.

It was the Gambino guy, Danny Bertelli, who had opened this door for me, and naturally I continued to have contact with him. During one of the meetings, I met a guy named Marco Barone, the owner of an auto body shop in Union, New Jersey. Barone started buying a lot of cigarettes from me, telling me, "Whatever you got, I can take it. If you got shoes, I can move shoes. Anything you got, I can move."

For his part, Danny Bertelli was a very cautious, old-school guy who studiously avoided talking about illegal business with me. Of course, that didn't mean he wasn't getting a slice of the action. Right from the start, I assumed he was making his cut off Barone's end, and Barone later confirmed that. I also knew that Bertelli was reporting back to Charlie on what I was doing with Barone, and telling him how much money I was making off the guy.

I was still dealing with Jimmy Smalls, but his usefulness to the undercover operation was in decline. That was primarily because I was now in solid with Charlie, but also because of his recent conduct. He had started hanging out with some Bloods and gotten himself arrested a few times. One of the arrests was for domestic violence.

It wasn't hard to guess that Charlie would not be too pleased about his nephew repeatedly bringing himself to the attention of the police, so for the sake of the operation, I started backing away from Jimmy. At the same time, I continued keeping Luigi on the hook, selling him mainly cigarettes, because he was a DeCav associate and there was always the possibility he could make a key introduction.

Overall, I had some balls in the air, I was getting the job done, and I was making money. That was the whole point of these activities: to build credibility with Charlie by showing him I was a reliable earner. I would sit on the phone with him for an hour or so most nights, talking about the day's work and letting him instruct me on how to conduct business and how to conduct myself on the street. As far as he knew, I had been a one-man gang up to the point we met. I made certain that he understood that I'd never been with another crime family and didn't know anything about Mafia life. In this way, I maneuvered him into teaching me about his world.

One of his familiar refrains was "You meet somebody new, Giovanni, you let him know. You let him know what *borgata* you're with, you tell him you're with the DeCavalcantes, and you stick our flag in the dirt. You gotta let it be known." Another lesson, oft repeated, was "Remember, Giovanni, be a piece of sand on the beach. You understand?" In other words, don't do anything to draw attention to yourself. Blend in, and be careful.

Sometimes I would play him. He'd ask, "So, you understand how this works?"

"Not really, Charl. What the fuck is a consigliere? What's a street boss? What's an underboss? Yeah, I heard about them. I watched the movies. But I don't know what it really means."

He would be frustrated, but he would always take the time to explain. It was clear that he wanted to groom me into what he wanted me to be, so I would play dumb, but not stupid, when I needed to. That's how I got information out of him about the DeCavs.

Over time, I changed my approach slightly by adding a light touch of ingratiation: "Yeah, I know that, Charl. I understand. But I just wanted to hear it from your point of view. I want to understand everything. You're the skipper."

"Naw, listen, my boy. You're steering the ship out there."

"Maybe, but you're directing where this ship is sailing. You're the real skipper. You tell me which way to go and I'll go."

Eventually, as business improved and it was clear to him that I was making money, there came the pitch from Charlie I'd been expecting: "Ah, I'm glad things are going well for you. Good, good. Listen, you're paying your bills, you got your girl." (I had told him I had a girlfriend I was living with in New York.) "All right, listen. It's good you're making some money. So what you do is . . . after everything's done, you know, you paid your rent, paid your phone, paid your bills, you send me a little bit. Send me a car payment. Send me what you can."

There it was. That was his way of telling me it was time to start kicking up.

15

LOVE AND WAR

THERE WAS ONE SERIOUS DRAWBACK to my growing relationship with Charlie Stango, and it was those long phone calls. Inevitably, this pattern spilled over into my home life, aggravating the already high level of friction between me and Anna.

There were times when I'd tell her, "I'll be home in ten minutes," but by the time I pulled into the driveway, I was on the phone with Charlie, or with Jimmy, or sometimes with the case agent. So I'd sit there talking, and my kids would be looking outside and telling their mother, "Dad's home!" But then I wouldn't come into the house for twenty or thirty minutes while I finished the call, pulled off my pinkie ring, went through my mental self-counseling ritual, left Giovanni Gatto in the car, and finally went into the house. By that time, everyone was eating dinner, or had finished dinner, and Anna would be angry. "You're home, but you're not home! Why do you even bother coming in? Go back outside and sit in your car!"

Or, we'd be in the middle of dinner and the phone would start ringing, and I'd say, "I have to take this call. I have to go downstairs. I'll try to cut it short."

We had a full finished basement in our house, laid out much like a separate apartment. It helped to go down there because I could mentally check out of my house. Even if my kids weren't home, I couldn't face the "disconnect" of talking to Charlie while I was sitting upstairs in my real house. By retreating to the basement and locking the door, I was trying to avoid cross-contaminating my personal world with Charlie's world.

While talking to Charlie, I'd make it sound like I was in my apartment in New York. I would go down to the finished basement and make it sound like I was just getting home. "Hey, Charl. Just walking in the door," and I would switch on the TV for some sound effects. The trouble was, when I finally went back upstairs two hours later, the kids had been put to bed, and Anna would be in a rage.

"Well, who the hell are you talking to for two hours? You just left work! Who've you been talking to? What are you doing? Why are you locking the basement door?"

To a certain extent, my behavior had begun to poison her thoughts, and she started to question my loyalty, thinking that I was messing around on her. She was a cop, and she knew that some cops used UC roles as a way to be unfaithful in their relationships. Knowing that environment and knowing how cops could be, she always had those little demons of suspicion.

"It was Charlie," I'd reply. "I tried to get rid of him, but he had all this stuff he wanted to talk about."

"How could you possibly talk to that guy for two hours?" she'd demand. "You already talked to him three times today, supposedly!"

And I'd say, "Well, Charlie's a talker. He loves to talk." I know there were times that she simply did not believe me.

I want to state very clearly that I was not unfaithful to Anna. On the other hand, I did have a fictional girlfriend, and sometimes I was at least able to use her as an excuse to gain some free time with my family.

Charlie believed I was living in New York with a girl named Lena. The task force had a female agent all lined up to play that role should it ever become necessary, but it never did. My story about Lena was that I had lived in Florida when we met, and I'd moved back to Atlantic City because I wanted to be close to her. What does every guy do? Follows a beautiful girl. At least, that was a concept that Charlie understood and accepted. I told him Lena worked as a personal assistant for some hedge-fund guy who spent most of his time overseas. The great thing was, her employer owned an apartment in Manhattan that he hardly ever used. Because Lena is always traveling around and doing things for him and his New York apartment wasn't being used, he had told her that she and I were welcome to use it.

I said to Charlie, "We only have to pay the cable and electric bills every month. We've got a $4,500 apartment for probably $500."

"What?"

"Yeah. It's a fucking no-brainer, Charl! That's how I'm living in New York. I couldn't afford to live in New York if it wasn't for Lena."

"That's good. That's some good shit."

In another conversation, I fleshed out the story a little bit.

"Yeah, Lena's out in California right now."

"Why?"

"This hedge-fund guy, he's does a lot of business out there. He stays mostly in London, so Lena's out in San Diego, doing stuff for him. That's why she's gone a lot of the time. And with me on the road so much, sometimes leaving just when she's coming home, we miss each other. It works out that way."

"Well, you know, you gotta try, my boy. Gotta keep her happy."

This background gave me a perfect opening some nights when I was in the car and he and I were on the phone. Charlie would be saying things like: "Don't piss her off, Giovanni! Don't get on the wrong side of that girl. Go home. Spend some time with her."

"All right, Charl," I'd say. "Rest easy. I'm getting home now."

I would often say that just as I pulled into my own real-life drive- way. I knew Anna would be pissed off if I stayed out in the car talking. So what I was saying to him was sort of true, and it was easy to own. "Yeah, Charl," I'd say. "Better let me go. If I'm on the phone when I walk through that door, Lena's gonna break my balls." I was referenc- ing some of the tensions in my own life, and that made it sound more genuine. Charlie would let me go, and I would pull off that damned ring, drop it in the cup holder, close my eyes, and try to reconsecrate myself as the man my wife had married.

Over time, I developed another little trick. If he called during din- ner and I had to head off to the basement, I would cut things short by making it sound like Lena was upset.

"What? What? Hold on, Charl, Lena's getting pissed because I'm on the phone. She's trying to watch— Hold on a sec." He thought I was in a studio apartment and my girlfriend complained because she was trying to watch some *Real Housewives* thing on TV. "I've got to go into the bathroom," I'd say.

"Naw, I'll let you go. Don't get her mad! Don't get her mad!"

So if I didn't want to talk for too long because I wanted to spend some time with my family, that's how I would sometimes do it. The bonus was that these bits of playacting gave Charlie nice little snapshots of my fictitious home life.

But it wasn't only the phone calls that were driving Anna crazy. Too often, when I finally did have an evening at home, with my phones set on silent, I'd just sit in front of the TV, zoned out, thinking about the operation, or Stango, or Gooms, or the latest swag deal. Anna would try to engage with me, try to raise family matters for discussion and decisions, but I would only be half-listening. This distracted, and at times dismissive, attitude would set her off.

"OK, you're late! I understand. You missed dinner! I understand. You missed the kids going to bed! I understand. But you're still not home! You won't even engage in conversation with your wife, who's been doing all these things for you while you've been crawling around the streets! So why the hell do you even come home? You're here, but you're not here! It's not fair! It's not fair to me, and it's not fair to the kids!"

16

CHARLIE'S WAKING NIGHTMARE

I THOUGHT EVERYTHING was going well with the operation, and it was—until it wasn't. One night, in late March 2014, I missed a 3:00 AM call from Charlie. He left a message: "Giovanni, this is Charlie. Whatever you know my nephew's doing, if it's against the law, I want nothing to do with it. Do me a favor, please. Don't set up my nephew neither. And do yourself a favor. Don't call me back anymore, OK? I want nothing to do with you, kid."

Obviously, this perplexing message had the potential to end the investigation.

I immediately tried calling Jimmy Smalls. He didn't pick up, so I decided to call an undercover coordinator within the Bureau. He was not my supervisor—I called him only as a friend and confidant. I said, "Listen, I just got this crazy message from Stango." I recited it back to him. "I don't know what this means."

He reacted with alarm. "Don't call him back! Don't call any of your targets! Don't do anything until I figure this out."

"I'll figure it out on my own. I'm just calling to ask what you think I should do. Give him a call? Wait another day?"

"No, no! Don't do anything! I got to make some calls here."

He inserted himself into the development as if he were my supervisor, and I didn't like that. After waiting a day, I went to the office and told him I was calling Jimmy Smalls. "I'm not asking you," I said. "I'm telling you."

After leaving Jimmy a few voicemails, he finally called me back. "What's the matter?"

"Your uncle left me this weird message." I told him about it.

"Fuck! I'll try to reach him. I'll call you back."

After a few hours, with nothing back from Jimmy, I got fed up and called Gooms Bertelli. "Danny, have you heard from Charlie? He called me up and left this crazy fuckin' message." I recited it.

"What? No, I ain't heard nothing like that, Giovanni."

"Did you hear about anything that went wrong? Guys saying I did something to him?"

"No. Nothing. I'll call him and find out."

Pretty quickly, Danny phoned back and told me about a strange conversation he'd just had with Charlie. After asking what had happened with me, Charlie told him he wanted nothing to do with me anymore, without offering any real explanation.

All I could say was "What the fuck, Danny? I don't get it! I didn't do nothing to him!"

"He'll probably calm down. He gets that way. He's fucking crazy, Giovanni. You should know him by now. He was locked up for too long. I'd say just forget him for now."

This turn of events ignited an internal war within the FBI. Ray, the lead case agent, agreed with me that we should keep going, but the undercover coordinator dissented. By expressing safety concerns, he had thrown up a red flag. Needless to say, the atmosphere became pretty tense between me and the coordinator when he walked into Ray's office and told us, "This case is over. We're shutting it down. It's a safety issue."

I said, "We've got to figure this out. The guy didn't chop me up into pieces. I'm still standing here."

And he said, "Well, this is bad. We can't take the chance. Your safety is my responsibility. I could be held liable." (Translation: *I need to cover my ass.*)

At this point, my own case supervisor, Anthony Zampogna, got involved. He waded in and fought tooth and nail to keep the investigation alive. Zampogna was a transplant from New York's LCN squad. He had lots of experience, and he was fully alive to the valuable possibilities of our case.

After a week of this infighting, I got fed up and accepted an invitation to teach an undercover class at Quantico. While I was there, out of the blue, I started getting calls from Charlie. I wasn't allowed to have any contact with him, so I let the calls go to voicemail. But the man kept calling, again and again, and his tone was constantly changing:

"Giovanni, it's Charlie. Call me back!"

Or "Giovanni. It's Charles Stango. Call me back when you get this message."

Or "Johnny Man! It's Charlie. Call me back! Call me back, kid!"

Finally, after three days of this, somebody in the FBI hierarchy showed some spine and made the right decision. I was told, "OK. You can have contact."

When I answered Charlie's next call, I had already made up my mind to play him.

"Hello?"

"*Jesus Christ!* What the fuck? I gotta get an act of God to get you to answer the phone!"

"Who is this?"

"What?"

"Who the fuck is this?"

"It's me!"

"Well, who the fuck is 'me'?"

"What? It's me! Charlie!"

"Oh? Yeah. Hey, Charlie. What's up?"

"What the fuck? You don't know it's me!"

"I erased you off my phone. It came up unknown number, so I didn't know it was you."

"What the fuck? It's me!"

"Listen, I didn't call you. I didn't call you."

"I know. You didn't get my messages?"

"Naw. I haven't listened to any messages."

"Jesus Christ, been calling for like two, three days. I didn't know what happened to you."

He was ignoring the elephant in the room. I wasn't going to let him get away with that. I played the victim card: "Hey, Mister Stango, I get it. I got your message loud and clear. I didn't call you. No disrespect, but, you know . . . I'll change my number, but I don't want any problems."

"Naw, Johnnie. I wanted to talk to you."

"Yeah, I got your message you left a while ago. Got it loud and clear. I don't want any problems. Apparently, I did something to offend you. I don't know . . . I mean, what it was, and I . . . you know . . ." I purposely stumbled on my words. "I just don't . . . I don't want any problems."

"Naw, naw. Hear me out. Shut up and listen. That night I called you . . . I had a nightmare. I woke up in the middle of the night and I was staring at the fan, the ceiling fan, and the fan's spinning, and there's you, Giovanni, hanging off the ceiling fan, with a bunch of wires hanging off you, and they're connected to some other guy. And they're spinning around. I stumbled out of the bed, and I was yelling, and I went downstairs and got a drink of water. Then I picked up the phone and called you and left that message. Listen . . . I already talked to Danny, and I already talked to Jimmy. A thing like that happened to me one other time. I had an episode like that in the can . . . a crazy episode when I was locked up. I get that way, you know what I mean, kid? I'm gone. Shot out. Fucking bots."

"What's that have to do with me?"

"I had a bad dream! Listen, I don't apologize for nothing I do in the world. I don't fucking apologize to nobody for nothing, you understand me?"

"Yeah. I get that."

"OK? I don't apologize to no one, but from the bottom of my heart, my boy, I'm sorry."

I made a show of letting out a long, relieved breath. "OK. Hey, you know, I appreciate that. I do. I really do appreciate that, Charlie."

"Yeah. I was a little fucked up. I got a little stupid. I'm yelling, and Patty's grabbing at me, and . . ." Now he started rambling, almost as if he was drunk, and I couldn't understand half of what he was saying. "Patty was grabbing . . . I'm out of the bed . . . she's chasing me. What the fuck! Didn't know what was going on. She's trying to pull me back into bed and screaming at me, and I go downstairs. I had this episode, and I was a fucking mess. You know, what're ya gonna do? Listen. It is what it is. I don't know where the fuck it came from, but, you know, if you want to do your own thing, go your way, OK. But if you want, we can put this behind us. Let's put it behind us, my boy."

"Charl, listen, I don't know, you know, I just don't want any headaches, man. You know, I'm willing, but I didn't know what I did. I fucking panicked. You left me that message, fucking crazy, Charlie. Crazy shit."

"No, no. I apologize."

"OK."

"Listen, you gotta come out here, Giovanni. Come out to Las Vegas. We got a lot to talk about."

"You want me to come to Vegas?"

"Yeah, yeah. Come to Vegas. Come soon."

By the end of the call, I had received not only an apology from Mafia capo Charles Stango—a rarity in itself—but also what appeared to be a sincere invitation to visit him in Las Vegas. Now I just had to convince the Bureau to let me go.

17

LAS VEGAS

May 2014

WHEN I TOLD THE BUREAU about Stango's invitation to Las Vegas, I was immediately met with stiff resistance. The safety issue was still uppermost in everyone's mind. But I was determined. All my street instincts told me that Charlie wasn't setting me up, that he was preparing to bring me into the family—maybe even go on the record for me, and maybe, one day, help get me made. Whatever Charlie had in mind, I was ready to play the part.

The trouble was, I lacked real influence. Although I was the primary UC in the investigation, I was still just a TFO—a local cop assigned to an FBI operation. The "Bureau-cracy" made all the big strategic decisions, and all I was getting from the higher-ups was "You're not going to Vegas! You're not going to be around this guy. You're not going to his house. He could kill you."

We had to fight for it. My supervisor, Anthony Zampogna, believed in my ability to do my job, so once again he stuck his neck out. He didn't do it just for me but for all of us on the team, and to his enduring credit he got the required approvals.

The blueprint for the visit that Zampogna sold to the bosses was this: I would take Tommy with me, we'd book into a penthouse in a hotel right on the Strip, and we'd have Charlie Stango come there. We wouldn't leave the Strip, we wouldn't go anywhere with Stango, and we definitely would not go to his house. (He was living in Henderson, Nevada, right next door to Las Vegas.) We'd stay close to the hotel so my security team would always be within easy reach.

This visit would give me a chance to test the waters—to test my bond with the capo.

As soon as we checked in at the hotel, I called Charlie. I could tell from his voice that he was excited that I was out there.

Before he could ask me to come to his house, I headed him off. "My buddy Tommy's out here with me. He's my money guy. He's got some business out here with an associate, so I'm here on his dime." This story had the value of sending Charlie a message not only that I hadn't made the trip solely to see him but also that I wasn't using "our" money from the swag sales to pay my travel expenses.

"OK. Sounds good."

"Yeah, Tommy's got this guy who has a place up here. A penthouse! It's unbelievable, Charlie. You gotta see it—$2 million, right on the Strip!"

"Oh? Yeah, yeah. Gotta see that."

"Yeah, come on over. We're going to get a cabana outside. We're going to watch the Kentucky Derby, so come, and bring your suit. Spend the day."

But when Charlie showed up in the hotel lobby, carrying his swimsuit and flip-flops in a little brown briefcase, I'd already decided it was time to change the dynamic. We had planned to show off this humongous penthouse we were using, but I said, "Fuck that. I'm not showing him anything."

When we met in the lobby, Charlie was bubbling. "So, top of the building, eh? The penthouse?"

"Yeah, it's gorgeous, but we're not going up there."

His face fell. "Why not?"

"Tommy's up there. He's got some girls from the last night. Been partying like rock stars. Place is a mess. Broads all over and they're smoking weed. I don't want to expose you to that shit, Charlie. You're on paper, and we can't take the chance." By "on paper," I was referring to the fact that he was on federal probation.

"Oh, yeah. That's smart thinking, Giovanni."

"If you want to get changed into your suit, you can use the locker room downstairs."

So, yeah, I treated him like a bit of a jerk, but it worked in two ways. I showed him I was looking out for his interests, but I also showed him I wasn't just some bootlicking wangster. (That's what we call gangster wannabes.)

As I had told him, we'd rented a cabana by the pool. Tommy wasn't around for most of the day, allowing me and Charlie to sit out there together, sunbathing, ordering drinks and food, and watching the Kentucky Derby.

At one point, as I was moving around, arranging for more drinks and some food, he slapped my lounge chair with his hand and said, "Sit down! I want to talk." So I sat, and from then on he was just grabbing at me, saying things like "We got good things going on here. It's gonna be a good thing. We're going to make money." He leaned closer. "I'm glad Tommy's not here. I want to talk to you about our thing."

"The thing we're doing with the cigarettes?"

"No. Our thing. This thing that you're coming into."

"Oh. OK."

"I want to lay it all out in person now that we're here. I didn't want to talk on the phone, understand?"

"Yeah."

"OK. I tell you to fly the flag, it's for the *borgata*. You know what a *borgata* is?"

"Yeah. Like, the cradle. The family."

"Right. Now listen . . ." And for the rest of the afternoon, Charlie explained the entire structure of the DeCavalcante family and its relationship with the Gambinos.

"I'm going to hook you up with guys," he promised. "I'm going to really start piping you in, kid. I'm going to start making calls. When you get home, you're going to hit the ground running."

I had told him earlier that my girlfriend, Lena, and I had recently moved into a different apartment in the city, near Mulberry Street—John

Gotti's old stomping ground in Little Italy. He loved it. "Ah, you're right by my guys. It's perfect. I can plug you in."

We had a good day. We watched the Kentucky Derby, sitting side by side, talking real close. Tommy came down at one point, and I introduced them. Charlie liked Tommy, and he was clearly comfortable and relaxed. He must have felt safe because, sitting there in our swimsuits, shirts off, sweating our asses off in the heat, there was no way I could be an informant or a cop wearing a wire.

From an investigative standpoint, it was an extremely fruitful conversation. But more important for the long game, Charlie and I connected in a deeper way during that afternoon. To understand why he latched on to me so quickly, squeezing my arm, patting my back, you have to understand where "Giovanni Gatto" came from. I didn't put on a Halloween mask. I was just me. No, I didn't tell him my real last name, and, yes, I lied about having a criminal history. But when we talked, I was genuine with him. I was open with him, and we shared our feelings about certain things. Yes, I was playing a role, but I only needed to be myself to make the bond with him grow. Charlie made it easy, because this version of Giovanni was a product of my personal background.

I am the first to admit that if I'd made different choices at a young age—if I'd chosen to stick with my bad-guy friends—I would have become that other Giovanni. I could easily have ended up as some crime boss's right-hand man. Giovanni Gatto was, and is, the dark mirror image of myself. He's always been hiding inside me, but in my real life he comes out in different ways. Sometimes in constructive ways. He's been known to step in, not necessarily in a strictly law-abiding way, when he has encountered someone being bullied or abused by others. And sometimes in short-tempered, irrational, and destructive ways, as Anna and our children can attest.

My life as a cop also partially informed this Giovanni character. The things I saw in law enforcement—beatings, killings, people dying in my arms, *babies* dying in my arms, being stabbed, guys trying to shoot me, fighting for my life—I utilized and turned into "street." Charlie was a convicted murderer, and he never evidenced the slightest sign of regret about what he had done. My job was to impress upon this unrepentant killer that I too was capable of committing that ultimate act of violence.

I also drew on my relationship with one of my uncles. Mario was an old-school Italian guy who owned a trucking company. He knew a lot of hooked-up guys, but he never went over to the dark side. Talking to Charlie was like talking to Uncle Mario. They had the same ways about them, the same mannerisms, which made Charlie familiar to me. At some subterranean level, he responded to that aura of familiarity, and it made him want to be my mentor. I would sit there and listen and keep my mouth shut. By never talking over him, I showed respect. That's why he would sit on the phone with me for so long. A lot of my early tapes were just Charlie Stango teaching me, building me up to be who he wanted me to be.

That visit to Las Vegas began a whole new chapter in the operation. I felt like I was on top of the world. Charlie loved me, and everything was back on track. I'd gotten over the hump created by his waking-nightmare incident, and I'd proven my point to the FBI nonbelievers.

After Tommy and I flew home, Charlie continued calling me three or four times a day. Not only was he setting me up with mob contacts to help move swag, but now he was also talking endlessly about his plans for "legitimate" businesses.

"I got these companies out here, Giovanni! They're legit companies! I'm going to buy the Olympic Garden lounge. It's the only place in Vegas that has both gaming and strippers. I got some guys, some investors. It's all legit, you understand? So, what you're doing out there is on the back end. You keep doing the back end, and I'll keep doing it legit." (In order to keep his probation officer in the dark, Charlie was putting everything in the name of his live-in girlfriend, Patricia Malone.)

As time passed, I realized that some of his so-called legit projects occupied a whole other zone of unreality. I mean, some of it was completely over the top. As I learned later, he had some rich investor lined up who was supposedly going to bankroll all of his schemes. "We can move scrap metal! We can move blood diamonds! They're real diamonds, Giovanni! I went to the vault . . . seen them for myself! And bottled water! I've got an investor. We're going to buy a glacier!" Not surprisingly, the investor eventually got cold feet and bailed on him.

When I returned from that first trip to Vegas, I was exhausted. I decided to take a weekend off from all the craziness. I just wanted to relax, decompress, and spend some quality time with Anna and the kids. My preteen daughter was involved in a regional soccer tournament, and my parents were also planning to attend.

It was a near disaster.

18

TOO CLOSE TO HOME

THE SOCCER TOURNAMENT was held at a large outdoor complex in central New Jersey. The place was packed, with cars parked all over. With multiple fields and each team scheduled to play two games in the course of the day, there were always three or four games going on at once. Our daughter had just finished her first game, and we were planning to sit for a while and have a picnic lunch with my parents. While we were getting that organized, the kids were playing nearby with their friends.

I was sitting on a folding chair, with my back to one of the parking lots, when I noticed a guy walking toward us. As he got closer, I recognized him.

Danny Bertelli! Here?

I was dressed in cargo shorts and a T-shirt, looking nothing like Giovanni Gatto, and here was this Gambino heavyweight heading straight toward me and my whole family, talking on his cell phone and staring in my direction.

I wasn't certain if he'd actually registered that it was me, so when he swiveled his head to look to his right, I jumped out of my chair. Moving quickly, I circled into the crowd on his left.

Then I strode toward him, calling out, "Hey Gooms!"

He whipped his head around.

"Giovanni? What the fuck? Whaddya doing here?"

113

As soon as I reached him, I gave him a kiss on each cheek. It was not a ritual I would normally display before a crowd of suburban soccer parents, but Bertelli was accustomed to me showing him that kind of respect. And I had a much more pressing motive. I was praying that my eagle-eyed wife would catch the move.

I give Anna huge credit because she did spot the kiss and instantly realized what was going on. She rounded up our kids and ran them off out of sight. I learned later that when my son saw me talking to Bertelli, he wanted to run over and join us. My boy always wanted to be part of any "guy thing" that was going on. Anna had a bit of a struggle on her hands, making sure he stayed away from me.

Meanwhile, my parents were left sitting there, not knowing what the hell was going on. In a matter of seconds, everyone had bailed on them.

For me, the incident instantly became even more strained, because Gooms placed the flat of his hand on my chest, pushed me back, and pointed a finger at my face.

"Why are you here, Giovanni? You ain't got kids, and you live in New York! What're you doing here? *You following me?*"

"Jeez, Gooms! I came to watch a game!" My mind was roiling, trying to think of an excuse—any excuse. *Think!*

Playing for time, I asked, "Is Jodie playing?" I was referring to his daughter.

"Yeah." He raised his voice. "But I want to know what *you're* doin' here! Tell me what you're doin' here!"

"Listen. I told you. I came to watch a soccer game. The girl I used to date, her kid, she's playing in the tournament. She just played a game."

"What kid?"

"The girl I used to date. I talked about her before. The girl I was with before Lena. I told you about her at dinner."

"No, you didn't."

"Yeah. I'm almost sure I did. I'm not with her anymore, but her kid . . . I've known her girl since she was little. Dated her mom for a couple of years, on and off. The kid's father . . . he's in the joint. He's held down right now."

"Ah."

"So she asked me. This is her first big tournament. She asked me to come watch it."

"What team?"

"Oh, she's on one of those Edison teams. But her team's out now." I made that up, praying I wasn't putting my foot in it. I knew there were probably four Edison teams on the field.

"Oh."

I tried to redirect the conversation. "So, Jodie's playing, huh?"

"Yeah. She's just finished. She's playing on this field next." He pointed at a nearby soccer pitch, and added, "Her team's playing these people over here," and pointed at a bunch of kids who were all wearing identical team sweaters—very familiar team sweaters. Danny Bertelli's daughter was going to be playing her next game against my own daughter.

My brain was shrieking at me: *You need to disappear—fast!*

Gooms asked, "So . . . you gonna watch another game?"

"Nah. I'm outta here. When I saw you, I was looking for my car. I'm lost."

"What field was your girl on?"

"She was playing over there." I waved vaguely. "I want to get back to the city. As soon as I find my car, I'm gone."

"Yeah, probably better to go now. I've got another game, and it's gonna be crazy getting out of here later."

"OK. See you during the week."

"Yeah, I'm heading to my car. It's over here."

My eyes followed his gesture, and my stomach knotted up. Bertelli's car was parked right behind where my folks were sitting, right behind the chair I had been sitting in only a few moments earlier.

My mind flashed with memories of all the times I had seen Gooms arrive at meetings at the wheel of that car, all the times I'd sat in the passenger seat of that car. *How the hell did I miss that?*

I now realized why he hadn't recognized me as he walked in our direction. He hadn't been staring at me; he'd been staring at his car. It was a late model black Mercedes with a distinctive metallic tint on the windows. I hadn't even noticed it parked there, twenty feet from our picnic. I had been blissfully, stupidly unplugged, enjoying my family, and oblivious to my surroundings. I had not only endangered the entire operation, I had endangered my family.

I said good-bye to Gooms and got out of there. I just faded into one of the parking lots and walked away. Anna and I had always had a plan. She knew that if I just walked away, I would disappear and find my way home when it was safe. The plan was always there, but we'd never had to use it. I got out onto the main road and started walking. When I was a few miles away, I called her on her cell.

"Hey, obviously you know what happened, right?"

"Yeah. Are you OK?"

"I'm fine." I told her where I was. "You're going to have to send my dad. Send him to get me, would you?"

My father came to pick me up. When I got into his vehicle, he gave me a long, sorrowful stare. "What the hell is going on with you? Are you crazy?" He knew that I'd signed on with the Bureau, and he had a rough idea of the work I did, but he didn't know the full extent of it. Now he was sensing just how dangerous it was. He didn't yell at me, but deep concern was written all over his face. "How do you and Anna live like this? You guys shouldn't be living like this! This is bad. Really, really bad!"

He drove me home in silence.

Anna told me later how things had gone after I left the tournament. Painfully aware that our true surname was stitched across the back of our daughter's team sweater, she had spent the next game with her eyes locked on the man she had seen me with, alert to determine if he was paying any special attention to our child. After the game, she and our daughter walked over to a stall that was selling tournament paraphernalia. While they were there, Bertelli's wife and daughter came over to browse as well. The wife kept looking at Anna and our daughter—or so it seemed to Anna, who was by now feeling totally paranoid. Because of her police experience, and knowing what she did about my case, when she and the kids left the tournament grounds she didn't drive straight home. She took a long a circuitous route, keeping an eye in the rearview mirror, making absolutely certain that they weren't being followed.

The whole afternoon had been an agonizing experience for Anna, and it only served to amplify her fears about the danger my operation was posing to our family. She said to me, "Yeah, sure we had a plan in place, but I never thought it would ever be needed at one of her soccer games! Her team hadn't even been scheduled to play in that tournament. It was just a last-minute, random thing. If you could run into somebody in a place like that, which is entirely out of the context from our everyday life, we're not safe to go anywhere! The FBI never should have let you do this case! We live too close to these people!"

Again, there are those questions: Why didn't some supervisor pull the plug on me? Working this close to the city where I'd been a street cop? Working this close to my real home and real family? Why did they let me do it? I don't know.

In my arrogance, I was saying to myself, *Who else were they going to get? It's not like just any outsider could come along and infiltrate the New Jersey Mafia. I was familiar with everything. I was the perfect fit. I had navigated through this world my whole life.*

But there is absolutely no doubt about it: this operation posed a real danger to our family. Today, looking back, I cannot believe I put my wife through that.

But it wasn't just Anna. As our children have grown older and wiser, they too have come to understand what happened on that soccer field and its wider implications. Their memories of that day, and of the scary course of survival training they later received, are always with them. The fearsome knowledge of what might have been—all because of my obsession with the operation—doesn't just haunt me and my beloved wife.

To my everlasting regret, it haunts us all.

19

THE DOG PICKS UP
A SCENT

BACK ON THE JOB, things were going well. I was getting these daily calls from Charlie, and from a prosecution perspective, I was taping some good conversations that promised to jam him up pretty tightly in the end. He'd always ask, "How did everything go today? Have a good day?"

"Yeah, we had a good day."

"All right. You gonna send me something?"

"Sure. I'll send you a card."

I had begun by sending him $1,500 in cash, tucked inside a birthday card.

He called me right after that first payment arrived. "Next time, maybe you shouldn't send it in cash."

"Well, what do you want me to do? How am I going to get it to you? You want to open an account? I could send it to an account."

"Naw. Just send a bank check. Make it out to Patricia Malone."

So I started sending checks. That's how I did my kick-up to him—sending cashier's checks payable to Patricia.

Charlie would always call to thank me: "Hey, got your letter! Thanks."

"Yeah, we had a good week, Charl."

"Yeah, that's good, that's good. I really appreciated it."

Then one day he told me to go see a guy who owned an excavation company in central New Jersey. "He's a good guy. Go see him. He might be able to help you move some of them shirts."

So I started dealing with this guy, and with many others. Slowly but surely, Charlie was setting me up with people who were interested in moving our swag.

At the same time, I was hearing that there was growing unease within the DeCavs. The old man, John Riggi, was now well into his eighties, so it was inevitable that there would soon be some restructuring. It was pretty much understood that Charlie "Big Ears" Majuri was going to take the top chair when Riggi either died or stepped down. The question, as always, was whether there was going to be resistance.

I spoke to Charlie Stango about it, mentioning that I'd heard there was going to be "some movement on our team."

"It doesn't change anything for us." He and Big Ears were close, he told me, and he would stay on as capo. All would go smoothly. "It's a good thing," he said. "I stay who I am."

One afternoon, I received a call from Luigi Oliveri. He wanted to meet with me. In light of my budding bromance with Charlie Stango, I convinced Tommy that I was too busy and asked him to handle Oliveri so that I could concentrate on Stango. This rather unsubtle pivot was not my idea—I was against it—but it was what the case agents wanted, and they were in charge. Tommy called Oliveri to schedule the meeting, claiming I was too busy to join them.

The Dog wasn't having it. He insisted that I come along as well.

We met in the parking lot of a strip mall in Linden, New Jersey. Right from the start, I sensed that something was different. Apart from the ratty cloth cap, Luigi didn't have his usual ragtag look. He was all dressed up in new jacket and a little button-down shirt. He was plainly attempting to look a little more polished.

He also had different swagger about him. Right off, he zeroed in on me, asking in a sarcastic tone, "So, what's going on?"

"Nothing. I've just been busy."

"So, what's going on?"

"I've been busy. What do you mean?"

"Where you been? I ain't seen you. Where you been?"

"What the fuck? What's with all the questions?"

"I want to know. You been out in Vegas?"

"Yeah. Who are you to ask me where I've been?"

"Think I don't know? You were out in Vegas with Charlie."

"Yeah. So fucking what?"

As soon as I said that, his nostrils flared and he copped an attitude. "So, what are you doing with him?"

"He asked me to come see him. So I went. That's the way it is."

"So . . . what? So, you're gonna be with Charlie?"

"Yeah. He wants me with him."

"Ah! Really?"

"Yeah."

"I know you for how long? How long you been doing business with me?"

"What the fuck's that got to do with anything?"

"It's got a lot to do with it. How long you know me? You know me longer than you know Charlie, right?"

"What is this . . . little kid games? Yeah, I know you longer than Charlie. But that don't mean nothing."

"Well, you should think about what you're doing. You should really think about what you're doing."

"What're you getting at?"

"I'm just saying you should think about who you want to be with. Charlie's not the right guy."

"That's your opinion, but I'm with Charlie. So that's that."

He got irate, raising his voice. "Listen, you know what? You're just a civilian. I couldn't touch you. I can't touch you."

"What the fuck? I'm a *civilian*? What does that mean?" He was just standing there, glowering at me, so I stepped into his personal space and gave it back to him. "Look. I'm with Charlie, and that's the way it's gonna be."

He backed down. "OK, OK."

I threw him a life ring. "So let's talk about business. We've got some samples for you. Some Athleta and Ralph Lauren polo shirts. Want to look?"

We walked over to where we had parked. Tommy went to sit in the car while Luigi and I continued our discussion. I was trying to keep things friendly, explaining that my relationship with Charlie wasn't going to affect our business and that he and I could still make some good money together. My pitch was working, and he was starting to change his tune.

"OK, obviously, if we're gonna be in the same camp, you should know that those things you're doing with those other guys, it's all coming from me. That thing you're doing with those guys, Pali, Jimmy Smalls, and Mike, that's all me." We'd been buying a lot of coke from this Pali guy, who we'd met through Jimmy.

"Oh, yeah? The other stuff I was doing—that's you?"

"Yeah, that's all me. That's my stuff. Those are my guys. All coming from me and my crew."

He was obviously trying to impress me. The subtext was *You really should be with me, not that old guy Stango.* But at least our conversation was moving along in a decent tone, and I was starting to feel comfortable again.

And then everything went sideways. Tommy jumped out of the car and charged toward Luigi. "Give me your phone!" he yelled. He pointed at the phone on Luigi's hip. "Your phone! Give me your fucking phone!"

I said, "Bro, what's the matter?"

"Just give me your phone!"

Luigi handed over his phone, and as soon as he did, Tommy muttered, "Fuck! Fuck! Fuck!" and just walked away with it. He walked over to the mall and started walking back and forth, doing something with the phone.

Luigi was following him with a finger. "Where's this guy going with my phone? What's he doing with my phone, Giovanni? What the fuck is with this guy?"

"I don't know. I really don't know, Lou."

Luigi was enraged. "This guy's with you? Right? How long you know this fucking guy?"

Tommy ducked into a Verizon store. I later learned that he was begging one of the sales reps to help him delete a message.

Having no idea of this, I said to Luigi, "C'mon. Let's go see what the fuck's going on."

We walked toward the store, but before we arrived, Tommy came out. He looked stressed. Almost distraught.

I confronted him in front of Luigi. "What the fuck, man? What the fuck's going on?"

"G, we gotta go!" He handed Luigi his phone. "We gotta get outta here, right now!" Immediately I thought something had gone terribly wrong. But then Tommy blurted, "It's my kid! Something's wrong with my kid. We gotta go, now!"

I said to Luigi, "Listen, I'll call you later. As soon as I find out what the hell happened, I'll call you."

We got in the car and drove away. After a few minutes, out on the highway, I asked, "OK, what's the matter with your kid?"

"Naw. I just fucked up. I did something stupid. Real stupid."

"What happened?"

"I shot a text. I meant to send it to someone else, but I sent it to Luigi by accident."

While he'd been sitting in the car, Tommy had composed a text message to someone in which he made an unflattering reference to Lui the Mutt. Then he'd sent the message to Luigi's phone by mistake. It was just the kind of mistake that can get someone killed.

Seconds later, Luigi called me. "Tell me what the fuck's going on!"

"I'm still getting this fucking story from him, so let me figure this out." I hung up on him, and said, "Tommy, what were you thinking? That was really fucking stupid! Now we need to come up with a story to cover this."

"Fuck that guy. Fuck him!"

"Not good enough. We can't just ignore him. Maybe you can run and hide, but I've gotta go back to these people! I'm the one who has to answer for this. So we better start thinking about why you grabbed his phone!"

So, I came up with a story. I called Luigi back later and explained that Tommy's phone died just when his wife was in the middle of telling him that his kid had been in an accident. His phone had gone dead, so he'd jumped out of the car to get one of our phones. I told Luigi, "He just saw your phone and pointed at it."

"Well, why didn't he ask you for your phone, Giovanni? Why did he ask me for mine?"

"Because he didn't *see* my phone. He was in a panic, and he saw your phone on your hip and just focused on that and got stuck on 'Gimme your phone! Gimme your phone!'"

"Yeah? Well, he never even made a call on my phone!"

"I don't know. It is what it is, Lui. It's fucked up. We went to the hospital. His kid got stitches. I had to deal with it all. Listen, let it go. Let's move on. When do you want to meet again?"

I managed to put this whole shitstorm to bed—or so I hoped. But Luigi really never really let it go, and this incident would come back to bite me. Everything the Dog had wondered about me in the past—"cops trying to take a shot at us," people trying to infiltrate, and now this incident with his phone—just made him more and more suspicious.

Because of this incident and Tommy's carelessness, I dissociated myself from him, and from that day forward, I was even more careful about who I did business with. The gravest danger is to be suspected as a big mouth or a rat. In the mob world, I'd rather be outed as a cop than a rat. That's because for a rat, it's only going to end one way.

20

GAME OF CHAIRS

BECAUSE IT WAS INCREASINGLY CLEAR that the DeCavalcante family was on the verge of restructuring, the boss of bosses, who was pushing ninety, wanted to name his successor to the top seat before he died. But various factions within the family were not completely agreed on who should be next, and the uncertainty was starting to generate dissension. Incongruously, one of the primary causes of this internal tension was the Dog.

Luigi Oliveri had gotten himself made at a secret ceremony. When I heard that, I immediately understood why Luigi had displayed that big chip on his shoulder at our meeting in Linden. It explained the nicer clothes, the amplified swagger, and the warning that I should be careful about who I want to be with. He'd been trying to get me to come with him. He was starting to form his own crew, and I would have been a terrific asset, because I was an earner. He didn't have any earners like me.

Word got around that Oliveri had been sucking up to John Riggi, showing up every day at his house, bringing him coffee and pastries, and spending time sitting with him. Manny Riggi, the old man's son, was in thick with Oliveri and had been putting pressure on his father, telling him Luigi was a good and loyal guy and had been in the neighborhood his whole life. Manny told his father he should bump him up while he was still boss, make him a soldier. He kept urging him to do it before he retired and passed the torch.

Finally, John Riggi caved. He reasoned that since he was the boss, he could do whatever he wanted. He could make his own rules. So Manny got Luigi over to the house and escorted him into the old man's room. Riggi went through the ceremony right then and there, transforming Luigi Oliveri from an associate to a made member in the DeCav family.

Apart from the boss's son, there had been no witnesses from the family, which meant it was a completely irregular procedure. For all anyone knew, it hadn't even been a traditional ceremony—pricking the candidate's finger, dropping his blood on a card bearing the likeness of a saint, burning that card, and passing it from hand to hand, accompanied by speeches of honor and loyalty to the family.

On top of that, there had been no background check. If, for example, John Riggi had wanted to make up five associates, the procedure required him to put all five names on a list. Then a senior family member, usually a street boss or the consigliere, would take the list to each *borgata* (the families in the New York area) and ask if any of them had a problem with anyone named on the list. If nobody has a problem with a name, that associate would be clear to get made. If anyone had a problem with the guy—even some ancient grudge—then he could get pushed off the list. That didn't mean that he wouldn't get made at some later date, just not right now.

Many DeCav members were deeply upset by what the boss had done. Making Luigi Oliveri in that way had set a bad precedent. Big Ears Majuri and his crew refused outright to recognize the procedure. Majuri was poised to take the top chair, and he was closely aligned with solid, longtime mobsters such as Luca "Milk" Vitale and the consigliere known as "Shipe."

But unfortunately for Big Ears, there were too many abstainers for him to make a decisive move. Solid old-school mobsters in the family were telling him, "Sorry, I can't take your side right now, because the old man is still in the seat. Once he's not there, that's a different story, but for right now, I gotta be loyal." From their point of view, Riggi had been a solid boss, taking care of them over the years, and they owed him.

Charlie Stango was on the phone regularly with Big Ears and Milk, and they'd been feeding him day-to-day information on what was going on with the Administration. To put it mildly, Charlie was not happy about what he was hearing. One day, out of the blue, he called me with a quick and terse warning: "Listen, Giovanni. I gotta come to New Jersey. Gotta come back for a visit. I got called in." Then he added, "And while I'm there, I'm going to go on the record for you."

I was shocked, but I had enough of my wits about me to play dumb. "I thought I was on the record already. The flag . . . planting the flag."

"No. I'm going to go on the record for you with the Administration. I'm going in, and I'm going to let everybody know you're with me, and then I'm going to bring you in and go on the record with you." Just like that.

When I later explained what had happened to my FBI team, they loved it. Anthony Zampogna got very excited. "There's a chance you could get made! It's never been done. We've never had an undercover get made inside the mob!"

In that same phone call, Charlie told me that he had made a special arrangement with the owner of the excavation company in New Jersey. I was to be given an office in his building.

"I talked to him," he said. "He can help you out a lot. You shouldn't be running back and forth from New York to Atlantic City. That's a long ride for you. A long day. What you do is you set up camp in the middle—somewhere to call home base, somewhere to do all your meetings. This guy's place is where you can do that. He's got an office for you, with your own bathroom and stuff like that. That's what you need. He used to be with the Colombos, but now he wants to be with us. He needs us, Giovanni."

Charlie had obviously been muscling the guy, and that was fine with me. As a UC, I didn't want to get involved in muscling anyone, but Charlie had done it without even telling me.

"From now on, guys come to you," he instructed. "I'll send guys there and that's where you do your meetings. No more running around the streets, Giovanni. You understand?"

"Yeah. Yeah, I get it."

"We're building this thing up, and we're going to do it right."

I drove over to see the excavation guy, Mickey. He had a nice little office area for me, free of charge. It was perfect. I told him what color

I wanted it painted and what kind of desk I wanted—all the details. And he made it happen.

Mickey and I had already been doing some business, but now, with this development, I came to know him better. The thing is, Mafia connections aside, he was actually one of the sweetest guys you'd ever want to meet. Of course, he had his own issues (who doesn't?), and in his case they were anything but trivial. Mickey was a bit of cokehead, and because of that he was having a tough time holding his company together. Strangely, he didn't seem to care. He told me he was just in the business to make a bit of extra cash, and he was hoping Charlie would help him secure a few contracts.

So there I was, and I was riding high. My DeCavalcante capo had not only set me up with a nice little office of my own, but he was also going on the record with me.

What could possibly go wrong?

21

ON THE RECORD

October 2014

JUST AS CHARLIE was about to fly in from Vegas to walk me around and introduce me to the upper echelons of the DeCavs, the FBI operation ran out of case funds. By this point in the case, Ray had been transferred to another division and we had a different case agent. The new guy was thrust into the investigation quickly, and because our spending had exceeded its permissible limit, word came down from on high that we'd have to shut down pending an audit.

Charlie Stango's visit promised to be a huge step in the investigation, but now it all came to a sudden, screeching halt. An administrative request was submitted to headquarters, but in the meantime, I was told, "You can go ahead and meet with Charlie, but you can't spend any money—not our money and not your own money."

How was I going to play it cool—play the role of Giovanni the earner—*with no money?*

This was serious. Charlie was planning to take me out to dinner with a couple of the Gambinos—Gooms Bertelli and Nino Molinelli—and who knows who else, and I wasn't allowed to show them the proper respect. I wasn't even allowed to reach into my *own* pocket to buy these guys dinner or a drink. I couldn't spend a nickel.

As usual, it was left to me to figure out what to do. I called Charlie and told him I'd just received a call from an associate who had thirty cases of cigarettes, and I couldn't miss out on the score.

I said, "Listen, I know you're coming to New Jersey, I know you're coming to do your thing with me, Charl, but thirty cases is a lot of money for us! I've got to go out of state. I've got to go all the way to Virginia to pick up these cigarettes. I'm going to be held up for a couple of days."

He was OK with it. "Go do what you gotta do. You gotta earn. But be careful, right?"

That bought me a couple of days for the FBI management to get their shit together. Fortunately, the approval request went through, and I was given some money a few days later. I immediately called Charlie. He'd been leaving messages, and I hadn't responded, so he was worried—and angry.

"I tried to call you! Why didn't you pick up your fuckin' phone, Giovanni? I'm with these guys, and I'm calling, and you're not there, and that don't look good!"

"Charl! I told you what I was doing: picking up those thirty cases! When I do those things, I buy a burner phone. Then I go do it, and I trash the phone as soon as I get home. I'm never going to take my own phone with me. This way, they can't ping me and track me! You were trying to call me for three days, and my phone was on the coffee table in my apartment."

"Ah . . . good thinking, my boy. Smart thinking." He bought it, and he loved it.

He told me he was at Russo's Meat Market in Elizabeth, and I should join him there. When I climbed into my Escalade to make the trip, I was nervous as hell. I had it in my head that he was planning to go on the record with me as soon as I arrived. I felt like I was going to pass out. But, as I soon discovered, he only wanted to meet for lunch. We had a bite together, and he introduced me to a few of the guys who worked there.

Unknown to me at the time, Charlie wasn't quite ready to take the big step. It was one thing for him to say, "You're with me now, flying my flag," but it was a much bigger thing to go on the record with the DeCav-alcante and Gambino families for a relatively unknown street criminal who had already raised suspicions in certain quarters, not least with the recently "made" Luigi Oliveri. So, Charlie was asking, inside and outside the family, about me. He needed strong assurances that he wasn't making a mistake with me, and he'd been continuing his due-diligence inquiries ever since his flight touched down in New Jersey.

When we finished lunch, he had me drive him to the Holiday Inn in Clark, New Jersey, where he was staying. When I dropped him off, he instructed me to return and pick him up the next morning. What I later learned from Charlie was that, after I left, Nino Molinelli and Gooms Bertelli came to the hotel to meet with him. When it came to going on the record with Giovanni Gatto, Charlie was dotting the i's and crossing the t's.

When I arrived at the Holiday Inn the following morning, he was waiting for me outside. He was all dressed up in a leather jacket, nice slacks, shiny shoes, slick polo shirt—pure gangster style. His girlfriend Patricia Malone was there with him, and this was the first I'd ever seen her in person. She was in her forties, short and stocky and, during this initial encounter between us, pointedly standoffish. She had parked herself on a bench near the hotel entrance and was smoking a cigarette. She said, "Hey, Giovanni. Nice to see you," but she was very cautious, verging on unpleasant.

Charlie and I got into the Escalade, and he started telling me where to drive. As each turn brought us closer to his old neighborhood in Elizabeth, I could feel his mood changing. He became happier, somehow more fulfilled, more invigorated. He was going home, and the young gangster in him was coming out. "*Aaah.* I'm home. I'm breathing my air. I'm becoming me again, Giovanni."

As we were driving, he mentioned he'd spoken to Luigi.

"You talked to the Pet?" I was surprised.

"Yeah, I talked to him. I said, 'Hey, Lou, what do you expect to get out of this thing of ours?' I asked him point blank. 'You got your button. At least, you *think* you got your button. What are you looking to get out of it?'"

"What did he say?"

"Money. Strictly money. That's all it is to him. I gotta to tell you, the upper levels are not happy with him. He's surrounded himself with big thugs. But what are the thugs gonna do when Luigi goes? All them big guys . . . what are they gonna do when the shots start going off? All them big guys always run for the hills, Giovanni. Anybody starts shooting, they all fuckin' run. You can surround yourself with gorillas, but when the bullets start flying, they run away." After that, he went quiet.

I couldn't help wondering where that little speech came from. What was going on inside his head? What incident from his past was he reminiscing about?

We got to Russo's Meat Market and sat down for breakfast—the very traditional peppers and eggs. I quickly realized that the whole point was to occupy a table and let ourselves be seen. Guys kept coming in, calling, "Hey! Look who it is!" and coming over and giving Charlie the kiss. "Hey, hey! It's good to have you back!" But, with some of these guys, I sensed the nervousness behind the ritual greetings. They were saying "Hey . . . uh, Charl! Hey Charlie! So good to see you!" kissing him and making these noises, but their eyes were saying, *Fuck, I can't believe Charlie's back here. Someone's gonna die. Someone's getting whacked.*

While we were eating, this huge guy walked in. He was the largest human being you'd ever want to see. "He's a Zip," Charlie told me later. "From Sicily—we call 'em Zips." This character didn't appear to speak much English, but he made it clear he was starving. One of the employees behind the butcher cabinet told him, "Angelo, just relax. Five minutes. Five minutes it'll be ready."

Apparently, Angelo couldn't wait, so he pointed at four links of Italian sausage that were sitting on the butcher's counter—raw sausage.

Charlie grabbed my arm. "Giovanni, watch this!"

As soon as the butcher handed over the sausages, Angelo selected a link, bit off the end, stuck the skin tube into his mouth, and sucked the raw meat out of it. He ate all four sausages that way, sucking the meat down his gullet.

"See that?" Charlie said. "Dynamite guy, that Angelo. Great guy."

"Really? See what he did with that sausage?"

"Oh, yeah. He's an animal. Great guy, though. Do anything you tell him . . . kill anybody you want. He's like a machine. You gotta see him eating a sandwich while he cuts up a body. Eating a sandwich! He don't give a fuck. No heart and no brains."

"Yeah, Charl," I said, with just a hint of mockery. "He sounds like a real good guy." We both laughed.

When Charlie finished his breakfast, he started making a series of calls, telling people he was around. At one point he stepped outside, yelling into his phone. When the door swung shut behind him, Richie Russo, the guy who owned the place—looked over at me. "Hey, Giovanni! Got your hands full there. You know what you got into, huh?"

"What's that?"

"Beeps. Beeps is a fucking crazy man. He's gonna have you running. You got your hands full there, kid."

"Yeah, yeah. It's all right. I'll do anything for him. He'd do anything for me."

He shook his head. "Well, I'm just saying, you got your hands full."

With breakfast finished, we drove around the Elizabeth neighborhood and some of the surrounding area. Rain had been in the forecast, so before I picked up Charlie at the hotel, I stopped at a Target and bought an umbrella. I held it for him every time he got out of the car, playing my part, feeding his gangster ego.

We made a few stops along the way. He was reliving his glory days and letting everyone know that Charlie "the Hat" was back. It was also his way of showing me off. He wanted to make the best of our time together and plug me in as best he could—all for his personal benefit, of course.

One of our stops was at a shipping company in the Elizabeth area. Charlie told me I might have a use for the owner's services. I think the visit was a way for him to breathe down the owner's neck a little, just in case we needed to use his company in the future.

The owner was clearly taken aback by Charlie's sudden appearance, but he didn't seem at all intimidated. It was obvious that they shared some history and that the owner was well connected within the DeCav family.

Charlie introduced me. "This is my man, Giovanni." He explained that I would be stopping by from time to time when I was in the area. I was polite to the owner and, like a good soldier, kept quiet while Charlie was speaking. The owner nodded in an understanding way and handed me one of his business cards. After discussion about possible business opportunities, and a few laughs, Charlie and I left to continue his little welcome-back tour.

After a few hours of this, he asked me to take him back to the hotel. He had set up a meeting with the Administration for later in the day, and he needed to prepare for it. "Come back later on. We'll hash it out and go for dinner."

But when I returned late in the afternoon, Charlie still hadn't left for the meeting. Gooms Bertelli and Patricia were there, so when Charlie finally did depart, I stayed to wait with them.

Minutes became hours. By the time the wait had stretched to nearly three hours, Patricia was getting nervous. She tried calling Charlie, but he didn't answer.

"I'm scared, Danny," she said to Bertelli. "I'm getting really scared."

Patricia Malone and Danny Bertelli had a long history together. He tried to put her at ease. "Patricia, Patty, relax. Take it easy."

"I don't know. I don't like this shit! I don't like this life. You know, he does these things, and he wants this life, but it scares me, because you know what can happen."

"What's going to happen to him? He's with his lifelong friends."

She looked over at me. "Giovanni . . . listen to me. He has to be careful. You *really* have to look out for him, OK?" She was pleading.

"I will. I always will, Patricia."

One benefit from our long wait in that hotel room was that Patricia started to relate to me, started opening up. "You've got to watch him on your end," she insisted, "and I'll watch him on the other end."

"I'm always going to look after Charlie."

"No, Giovanni. You've got to watch him on that end, where you are, and I'll watch him on the end over here."

And then, to my astonishment, she started explaining how she was getting information. I finally understood how Patricia had been in a position to warn people that the cops were looking at them: there *was* a law enforcement leak—and Patricia Malone was the conduit.

She told us, "My girlfriends, they still work in law enforcement, and they get information. I used to work for law enforcement as well. I used to work on the transcriptions, and stuff like that, when they did wiretaps. And when our guys got caught on wires, I used to fudge the wires. I would erase the tapes. One of my girlfriends told me—that's why I knew when Charlie's nephew, Jimmy, and that asshole son of his, Anthony, were going to get raided. When they were going to kick down Anthony's door at his house in Toms River, I called him, and gave him three weeks' notice before he got hit. I told him you're going to get your door kicked in, that the DEA was is coming. But he didn't listen to me, and what happened, Giovanni?"

"I don't know."

"They kicked his fucking door in."

"Did he get arrested?"

"No. The asshole didn't have anything in there, thank God. But they kicked his door in. I tried to tell him, but he didn't listen to me."

I said, "Wow, you really got it pretty good, huh?"

"Yeah, yeah."

So, we kept talking, trying to keep it light, but Patty was still on edge. Gooms kept telling her, "Relax, Patricia. Nothing's going to happen to Charlie. Nobody's got the balls to do anything to Charlie. He's fine. Patty. Don't get yourself all worked up."

Finally, stressed out and exasperated, she stood up and said, "I'm going outside. I gotta have a cigarette."

After she left the room, Gooms said, "That's the way it is here, Giovanni. You know that, right? There's no love in this business. When it's your time, you won't see it coming. If it's your time, you'll just hear the *pop*."

Sitting there, with my guts churning, all I could say was "Man . . . yeah. Yeah, I know."

He wouldn't let it go. "That's the way it is. One day you're on top. Next day, you're in a hole. It's just the way it is. If it happens to me, I don't want to see it coming. I don't even want to hear the *pop*." He paused. "But Charlie, he's going to be fine."

After fifteen minutes or so, Patricia returned to the room, and not long after, to everyone's relief, Charlie showed up. He looked utterly exhausted. "Ah, Jesus Christ! I just ran a marathon!"

"What's the matter?"

"I need a drink! Give me a fucking drink!"

We started laughing—Gooms and I, both laughing at Charlie. "So that was some meeting, huh?"

"Gooms, you got no fuckin' idea! Meeting? Man, it was a fuckin' marathon!"

Apart from the laughter, I stayed silent. As much as I wanted to know what had happened, it wasn't my place to ask. I wasn't going to come out and say, *So, what'd you discuss?*

Charlie collapsed into a chair, and Patty brought him a drink. He locked on to me and said, "Let me tell you, son. You! You caused me some ass-ache today!"

"Me? How?"

"You, my friend. You were *the* topic of conversation tonight. I went to war over you."

"How's that?"

"Luigi."

"He was there?"

"Yeah. The Administration had a little thing with him outside. But I sat down with them, and I went on record with you."

Gooms gave me a grave nod, signaling his approval.

"We'll make that official tomorrow. But this Dog. This fuckin' Luigi! This piece of shit!"

"What happened?"

"First he wanted to argue about who had the right to have you in his crew."

That was easily understood. It all came down to greed. I had already demonstrated that he could make a lot of money, and each man had his own financial interests at heart.

"That got him nowhere. They shut him down and sided with me. So then he tried telling them that I was planning to whack him out. He claimed that one time, when I was up in my nephew's apartment after I got out of the can, I mentioned that I didn't like something he'd said.

Some of my nephew's gangbanger friends were there, and they went back and told him that I'd said I wanted to kill him."

"Where does that come from?"

"He makes this shit up. It never happened."

I was thinking that it probably did happen. It sounded exactly like the way Charlie often talked when he was around Jimmy Smalls.

Charlie said to me, "Look . . . I'm tired. Go home and get some sleep. Tomorrow we got a big day! Gonna be a good day. We'll go meet everybody, and we're gonna put you on record and make it official."

We said our good-byes, and Patty actually hugged me when I left. After spending all those hours with her and after hearing Charlie's account of the meeting, she and I were good. She had watched how I conducted myself and how I interacted with Gooms, and as far as she was concerned, I had checked all the boxes. From that day forward, I never had another problem with Patricia Malone. She never looked at me sideways again. I was family to her now.

Later that evening, when I was at home, I received a call from my case agent. He told me that another agent had a certain reliable informant that had reached out to him earlier that day. The guy said he had some information on Charlie Stango. As it turned out, this informant had been at the shipping company we visited earlier in the day. After we left the office, he contacted his handler. He said he didn't have specific details relating to any crimes or schemes Stango may have been planning, but he wanted to make him aware that Stango had been accompanied by some new guy named Giovanni. He told the agent that he had felt "very uneasy and intimidated by this guy, this Giovanni"—to the degree that he felt it was important to call and bring the visit to the FBI's attention.

Those three words, *uneasy and intimidated*, told me something: that I was doing my job.

———

The next day, when I was on the way to Russo's for the big event, Charlie called. He was there already, waiting for me. "Where are ya? Where are ya?"

"I'm here! I'm coming around the corner."

I could see him standing outside the restaurant with a couple of guys. He was on his phone. He saw me coming down the block and waved an arm. "I'm here!"

"I see you. Be right there."

There was only one parking space out front, but it was tight as anything. I mean, really tight. But, as stupid as it sounds, I saw Charlie pointing at my Escalade, and in my head I was hearing him say, *That's my kid! That's him right there!* They were all watching me, so I knew I couldn't circle the block. That would look weak. So, thank God I'm a good parallel parker because I nailed it in one shot. Boom, boom, reverse, forward—I'm in, I'm done, with just inches between my bumpers and the other two cars.

I stepped out, and they were all standing there gawping. As I walked over, I heard Charlie saying, "Ah, now, that! That is a true New York park job! Tell me this guy ain't from New York, huh? You gotta be able to park like that in the city. Look at that, look at that!"

One of the guys said, "You do things like that, huh?"

I put on my break-your-balls face. "Of course. Two shots. That's the way I do things."

"Yeah, yeah, yeah."

My little performance had been the perfect icebreaker, a great way to start the day.

Charlie introduced me to the two guys, both your stereotypical *Sopranos* foot soldiers. I don't even remember their names—just some of the neighborhood nobodies that were kissing Charlie's ass before I got there.

One of them said, "So, you're from New York."

"Yeah."

"Oh, where do you live?"

Charlie butted in. "Hey, shut the fuck up! We're going inside. Let's go."

As soon as we entered the restaurant, Richie Russo called out to me, "Hey! Morning, Giovanni!" as if I was a regular—all because of Charlie.

"How ya doing?"

"Sit down, sit down! I got your breakfast. You like it hot and spicy, right?"

"Yeah."

"Right, right. Give me two seconds." He whipped up a plate of sausage, peppers, and eggs and brought them over.

Charlie sat there wearing a big grin. He said, "This is gonna be a good day."

So there we were, sitting in the middle of the deli. I noticed a big, bald guy parked in a chair across from me—and that nobody else was coming in.

Then I realized why. There was a guy standing at the front door, and if somebody from the public wanted to walk in, that person was blocked. It was, I guess, a special day for Charlie, so he wanted to make sure the room was his. The bald guy, reading a newspaper, was Milk's muscle, as I learned later. The street boss was coming to meet me, and he wanted to make sure his man was already there when I arrived with Charlie. I guessed that Milk had instructed him to keep an eye on me, because he was clearly only pretending to read the paper. Mainly, he was watching me.

When he finally put his newspaper aside, I said, "You done with that?"

"What?"

"Are you done with the paper?"

"Yeah. It's not mine."

I picked it up and I started reading.

Charlie chuckled at me. "What are you doing, Giovanni? Reading the paper?"

"Yeah, Charl."

"Did you say hello? This is . . ." whatever the muscle's name was, which I forget.

"Say, how're ya doin'?"

"It's Giovanni, right?"

"Yeah."

"Nice to meet ya."

"Yeah, yeah. Nice to meet ya." I went back to reading the paper, like he was a nobody.

Not thirty seconds later, Milk walked in with two other guys. I could hear them coming, because guys outside were reacting to his arrival: a chorus of loud talk and shouts and "Hey, hey, hey!" I steeled myself for the big moment.

Instantly it was "Hey, hey, hey, Milk! What's up? What's going on, Milk?"—this time from everybody working in the deli. They were coming out from behind the counter, kissing him, fawning over him.

We got out of our chairs, and Charlie joined the ritual. "Ah, what're ya doin'? How ya doin'?" Two kisses. And then, "So, Milk, this is my kid. This is my kid I was telling you about, my boy Giovanni."

"Hey, Giovanni."

Milk was a huge individual. He stood well over six feet, pock-marked face, humongous nose, broad rounded shoulders—just a really big, intimidating guy. He came up to me, said hello, and basically just engulfed me. I'm no short ass, but I had to reach up to kiss him, just to reach his cheek. He sat down next to me, right up against me and leaning close.

"So, what are we doing? What's going on, Giovanni? Who are your people? Where are you from? What do you got going?" The whole time during his nonstop questioning, he was bouncing, bouncing, bouncing one of his legs, the knee going up and down nonstop. "We hear you got some things going on."

"Yeah, I got some things. Charlie can tell you."

"No. You can tell me."

As I tried to gather my thoughts, my gaze slid past Milk toward the butcher section of the deli. Hanging on the wall were cleavers, bone saws, huge knives, and all kinds of implements perfectly designed to chop a body into pieces. My jangled brain was already on high alert, and now I started watching for any sign that I was about to be dragged to the basement, laid out, and threatened with dismemberment.

I quickly refocused. "I got cigarettes. Good supply . . . and reliable. I got shoes . . . shirts . . . purses . . . stuff like that."

"Where do you get them?"

ON THE RECORD   141

I reeled off a few made-up names and suppliers.

"I might be able to move those things for you. Charlie told me you're gonna be around. Charlie tells me things are going to be good. Things are going to change. Giovanni's gonna be with us. I just wanted to make it official."

"I'm here to help."

"I'll be in touch with you. Get your phone out. Here's my phone number. Give me yours." When that was done, he said, "Any problem at all, you reach out to me. You're here now. You got a problem, you call me. Leave a message. I'll get back to you. If I got to talk to you, or if I got to talk to him"—nodding at Charlie—"I'll call you."

"All right. Sure."

"I'm going outside now. I've gotta talk to a guy."

And that was it: one, two, three, done. Over the course of the next hour or so, I was introduced to several DeCav associates and to a pair of legendary figures: DeCavalcante consigliere Shipe and a funeral director named Carl Corsentino, the son of the undertaker who, back in the 1920s, devised the infamous double-decker coffins used by the mob to make their victims' bodies disappear forever.

When we finally got into my vehicle and drove away, Charlie was bubbling with excitement. He wasn't as excited as I was. Federal task force officer "Giovanni Gatto" had just been made an associate of the DeCavalcante crime family.

22

TESTED

AFTER WE LEFT RUSSO'S, Charlie asked me to take him on another drive around the neighborhood. As he was directing me to turn here and turn there—pointing out where John Riggi once lived, where various DeCav mobsters lived, or buildings they'd owned—he kept trying to make a call on his cell phone. Whoever he was trying to reach wasn't picking up, and Charlie was saying, "Where is this guy?" Eventually, I heard him say, "Hey, how're ya doin'? I'm here. I'll be outside. Come outside. Yeah, see ya in a minute."

As we were rolling along, he pointed at a building. "See that? I lived there. My mother used to own that building. Make a left here."

I swung into the street he indicated. It was a dead end.

"Turn around and park facing that way."

I parked facing the main road.

Charlie said, "Stay here," and got out of the car.

"Where are you going?"

"Be right back."

He walked to the corner, stood there for a few seconds, and then just walked away, out of sight. I didn't know where he'd gone or what he was doing. After sitting there for ten, maybe fifteen, minutes, I was starting to get nervous. *Am I about to get whacked? Or is Charlie causing too much drama? Is **he** about to get whacked?*

Just as I was kicking these thoughts around, Luigi appeared at the corner. He stood there, staring down this dead-end street, looking straight at my car. He pointed at me and gestured: *Come here!*

Now I was even more apprehensive. *What the fuck? Where's Charlie?*

I got out of the car and walked over to him. I was on my guard now, but seeing the anger on his face, I decided to play it safe. Pretending I'd just found out that he'd got made, I gave him the kiss and said, "Hey, I hear congratulations are in order."

"Walk with me!" he ordered. He was plainly agitated about something, and I noticed he was keeping his hands in his pockets. That was doubly worrisome, because I knew he always carried a .38.

"Where's Charlie?"

"Just walk."

Now I was on high alert, thinking, *Has he killed Charlie, and now he's going to try to kill me next?*

We started walking, and he immediately started in on me. "Before you start talking to somebody, Giovanni, you oughta find out who the fuck you're talking to. I'll chop you up into fucking pieces."

"What are you talking about?"

He launched into this whole big thing about how the last time we had met, I had disrespected him and how I'd been cold and sarcastic with him. But it was more than that. "That friend of yours, that thing he did with my phone—he took my phone, but the thing is, he didn't make any calls on it. Not one call! He didn't dial! No calls out!" He grabbed my arm. "Why didn't he use your phone?"

"I don't know. Honestly, I don't know."

"And another thing I didn't like. You guys left, and whatever happened . . ." He scowled at me. "If you're wearing a fucking wire, it is what it is."

"What the fuck you talking about, if I'm wearing a wire?"

Just at that second, a car pulled up with two guys in it. And a couple of other guys popped out of doorways and set up on stoops. They were Luigi's guys, and it was clear they were there to keep watch on him—and on me.

This asshole wanted me to answer for his suspicions, and I was boxed up in the middle of his neighborhood. This was either going one way or the other, because I had no way out. I was unarmed, and I had no eyes on me, and no ears on me. (I was wearing a couple of recorders, but no transmitter.) Whatever happened, I would be on my own.

So I stood there and listened to him rant while I weighed my options. I needed just the right balance. I knew I had to appear to take my licks, but at the same time, I couldn't be a pussy.

"If you're wearing a wire . . . !"

"I'm not wearing a wire! What the fuck! Listen, man, I just don't know what's going on between me and you."

"I'm gonna tell you, 'cause when you and that Tommy guy left, I had guys out there, watching. I went to go back to my car, and I'm carrying those shirts you gave me, and my guys got to me on my phone. 'Don't come back to the car! It's hot!' So I ducked into Home Depot and waited a few minutes. Then I came out, and I got in the car with my guys. I said, 'The girl in that car right there . . . you say she's been here the whole time? OK, follow her! If this guy's setting me up, I'll put him in pieces.' So, when she drove away, we followed her and we stayed on her, and guess where we followed her to, Giovanni?"

"I don't know."

"Guess where we followed her to!"

"I said I don't know."

"Fucking FBI building."

"FBI building. Yeah, and . . . ?"

"Either of two things: One, you're a rat—"

"No!"

"Hear me out! Hear me out!"

I knew what I had to do. I changed my demeanor and got cold and hard, because I knew he was watching me carefully, and his gorillas were watching me. He had his gun hand in one pocket and a set of keys rattling in the other. I figured the keys were going to be a signal. If I swallowed, if I stuttered, if I blinked, licked my lips, broke a sweat . . . I'd be screwed. So I just snapped into anger mode, took a step closer to him, and hissed, "No! *You* listen!"

"You gonna let me finish?"

I had already decided I wasn't going to let him finish. "You mother-fucker!"

Coward that he was, he wavered. "Or . . . you got heat on you, and you brought it to me."

"No!"

"Then your guy Tommy—"

I cut him off again. I knew that Tommy and Oliveri had never been arrested, never been put in cuffs, never been locked up. So I used that to my advantage. "Listen to me! Tommy's not like me and you. He's not like us. He ain't never done nothing bad. He's never been locked up. You understand? So, for him, I apologize. OK. I apologize for Tommy, but he's not like us."

I was telling him that I'd been to jail, that I'd done time. I was challenging him, and it worked. He visibly shrank. He was suddenly demoralized, and his whole demeanor stalled and faltered. I knew I had him in a corner.

I followed up by throwing him a bone, giving him a way out. "Listen, man. You know, it is what it is. I don't know how things went bad between me and you, how things are getting wrong. I always liked dealing with you." I turned to his favorite subject. "Your money was always good."

"Yeah, I had no problems." He was looking distracted, but he was calming down. "If we can get back to that . . . but, you know . . ."

At that moment, I noticed Charlie walking toward us, talking on his phone.

"See this guy here?" Luigi said, referring to Charlie. "Talk about heat! He's the hottest motherfucker out here. See what he's doing? Talking on the phone. He's always on the phone, and he's gonna get himself caught again. So, I'm thinking to myself, *You're talking dirty to me on the phone all the time—all the time. It's dangerous.*"

Charlie reached us, and Luigi stopped talking. At the same time, some guys were shouting from passing cars, "Hey, Charlie!" and Charlie was yelling "Hey! Hey, how ya doin' buddy? Bap, bap, bap!" and then he was saying to us, "Fucking love it here. Love it! It's my neighborhood. I grew up here. That's my building, right there! Love it here!"

After Charlie quieted down, Luigi turned back to me. "Yeah, well, you got cigarettes? You still got cigarettes?"

I made sure Charlie was listening and replied, "Yeah. I got some."

"You got the greens? You got the Newport menthols?"

"Naw. I don't have them. They're hard to get. But I've got a case of the red and a case of the white."

"All right."

"But, you know . . . the price just changed. Went up a little bit."

He snorted. "Hah! I bet." He knew exactly what I was doing, and more important for me, so did Charlie. I was taxing Luigi's ass. Surcharging him for insinuating that I was no good, that I was a rat.

"They're really good." I stared straight at him.

"Yeah, yeah. Whatever. Well, I need 'em. . . . I'll come by."

"Call me."

"All right. See ya later."

Charlie and I walked back to my Escalade. I couldn't help thinking that he must have arranged this entire confrontation with Luigi as a test—serving me up to a known antagonist to see how I handled myself. If I was right, there was a really good chance that the Dog had pitched all his suspicions about me to Charlie. If that was the case, I needed to get ahead of them. What if, during their walk and talk, Luigi had told Charlie about him and his guys tailing the female FBI agent? I had never told Charlie the story about Tommy's freak-out in the parking lot—about him grabbing Luigi's phone but never making a call. So now he might be thinking I'd been holding back on him. I had to deal with all of this head-on before it lodged in the back of Charlie's brain and mutated into another one of his crazy nightmares—or worse.

As soon as we got back in the car, I started yelling. "You hear that fucking guy? That fucking man! I am fucking pissed!" I laid it on. "Did you hear his fucking story, Charl? Listen, I bit my lip! For you, only for you, I bit my lip! Only for you! That was hard."

"I know you did," he answered calmly. "I know you did."

"Did you hear what this guy said? He followed a car, some fucking girl, and followed her back to the FBI building. What the fuck is that? How many times did you tell me, 'Don't come down to this neighborhood?' How many times did you tell me to stay the fuck away from this place because of all the heat they got now?"

I purposely ramped up my rage, steering with my left hand on the wheel while I punctuated my words by waving my right index finger in his face, or poking him on the thigh. Meanwhile, I deliberately made wrong turns, because I wasn't supposed to know my way around the neighborhood. "And, goddamn it," I shouted, "you were right! And now he tries to blame me, and make *me* out to be a bad guy!"

"Wow, Giovanni, that's some wild shit, huh?" He was still strangely calm.

"Yes! Crazy!"

"Yeah, yeah. Listen, a couple of weeks ago this kid was at my nephew's house, with a bunch of gangbangers, yapping, yapping, making up shit about me, and telling everybody shit. And I got through it, and now you got through it. So we move on. We carry on. But know what? Maybe this guy Luigi's wearing a hat too big for his head. I told him, 'Lou, you go be your own don.'" Charlie went quiet for a second, and then he added, in a quietly sinister tone. "There's always a place, and there's always a time."

I soon came to understand the genesis of his last remark. The DeCavs had recently put on a social event in a catering hall, not only for crime family members but also for outside relatives, including dozens of children. Luigi had walked in, full of self-importance, now thinking of himself as a made guy. An old-school gangster named "Tin Ear" Sclafani, a former enforcer for the family who was now past his day, had been sitting with his walking cane when Oliveri strutted past him. The old man lifted the cane and poked Oliveri in the belly. "Hey Luigi, look at you! You're getting fat like your brother!" (Luigi's brother was an extremely heavy individual, three to four hundred pounds.)

Luigi exploded, yelling and cursing, showing no respect for the old mobster in front of his wife and grandchildren and the other old timers sitting nearby. "You fucking old men! You don't know what's going on. Things are changing around here, and you better start fucking respecting me!"

Not surprisingly, members of the incoming Administration were extremely angry about Luigi's behavior. Charlie told me that Big Ears and Milk had visited him at his hotel room and told him about the incident. His reaction had been "The kid's out of control. We've gotta do something about him."

Their response was "Yeah, but there's gotta be a problem—a real problem. We want to do something, but not right now. Now isn't the time."

Charlie was furious that they would let Luigi get away with such conduct. He believed it would only attract negative attention from the other families and, potentially, unwanted attention from the cops.

He was determined to do something about it.

23

THE BONDS
OF INIQUITY

ONE OF CHARLIE STANGO'S SONS, Anthony Stango, lived in Brick Township, New Jersey, fifty miles south of Elizabeth. One evening before Charlie returned to Las Vegas, he told me I didn't need to drive him around the next day because, as he put it, "I'm going to see my kid."

Until now, I had been only vaguely aware of this son's existence. From random comments, I knew his street name was "Whitey," and from task force research files, I knew he was a convicted drug offender. During his visit, Charlie must have told Whitey about me, about what we had going on, and where I was setting up my office. And the son must have told his father he needed a job, because a few days after Charlie flew home, Mickey, the excavation company owner, told me that Anthony Stango would be coming to work for him has a truck driver.

The first time I met Whitey, I instantly realized why he had that nickname. His blond hair was so light in color, it almost looked bleached. I was also surprised by his size—he must have weighed close to three hundred pounds. He seemed nice enough, and he was respectful to me. But in many ways, he reminded me of his cousin Jimmy: half street thug, half wangster. In other words, a guy who didn't know what he was. I later learned that Jimmy's mother was Charlie Stango's sister, and that she had died young. Jimmy and Whitey had grown up together, almost like brothers, which I suppose partly explains their similarities.

I encountered Whitey at the excavation company almost every day. I had a pretty good idea he was reporting back to his father, so I kept showing my face there, bumping into him and Mickey, going out to lunch with them, but always making sure I appeared busy. I was constantly making it look like I was picking up swag, moving swag, selling swag, saying, "I gotta run. Got this deal . . . I'm running here . . . gotta run there." To complete the picture, I started leaving boxes of swag and cases of cigarettes in my office. Then I would say to Whitey, "Hey, you know what you can do? Do me a favor. Break these all down, take these shirts, put all the small sizes in one box, all the mediums in another, same with the large." With Whitey and Mickey noting the constantly changing products and brands and hearing me talk about these runs, I was pretty sure news of all this would find its way back to Charlie's ear.

Of course, it was all fake activity. My underworld version of performance art.

It wasn't long before Whitey started saying things like "So listen, Giovanni, if you need any help, if you want me to move some of this stuff like Jimmy was doing, I got connections. I can help."

"Yeah, yeah. I'm good, thanks, Anth. I'm good. Just drive the truck for Mickey. Just do what you're doing."

But he kept angling to get in on the action, and soon I started getting pressure from Charlie to bring Whitey on board. "If you need anything, Anthony is there. Just ask him if you need help with anything. He's there for you."

"Yeah, yeah, OK. Thanks, Charl."

"He's into some green stuff," Charlie told me. Meaning marijuana. "He's selling that stuff. He's got people."

"Well, if you want me to. You really want me to give your boy some of our stuff to sell?"

"Yeah, yeah. Let him run around. He's got the truck. He can sell it right off the truck."

"OK."

So I started piecing out some product to Whitey, but as he became more involved, he started bringing some of his friends around. That was fine up to a point, but none of this low-level activity was going to do much to advance our operation as a serious LCN investigation. I needed to figure out a way for me to get away from these street kids and spend more time with my capo. The problem soon became a topic of discussion at the task force level, and it was agreed that I should start making regular trips out to Las Vegas.

Planting the seed, I told Charlie that things were going really well, and I wanted to fly out and pay him his kick-up in person. He liked that.

Traveling back and forth was going to be costly, but I did have a lot of street money available to finance the trips. The Gambinos were buying a ton of stuff, mostly cigarettes, as was Sammy Cigars, the associate who owned the auto body shop, along with another associate of that family. I would sometimes have a hundred cases of cigarettes come to me, and they would be gone in a few days. There was always money coming in, so I was able to start traveling out to Nevada on a fairly regular basis. I would pay Charlie his kick-ups—usually two or three grand in cash—spend some quality time with him, and come away with some extremely valuable recordings for the investigation.

These frequent visits had the added effect of taking our relationship to another level. For example, Charlie began having what I call "empowering talks" with me. These were those fatherly be-the-man-you-were-born-to-be conversations. Yes, he was manipulating me, because it was all for his benefit, but that wasn't his only motivation. On one trip, he initiated a conversation about me killing someone or doing some serious damage to somebody. He said, "Listen to me . . . even if you're wrong, I'll make you right. Even if you kill some guy by mistake, or you kill him on purpose but you fuck things up and almost cause World War III—even if you're wrong, Giovanni, I'll make you right."

I looked into this old gangster's eyes and saw . . . sincerity. It was then that I knew I had gotten way past the get-to-know-you phase of this covert operation. Charlie Stango truly cared about me. That helped my peace of mind in my undercover role. Knowing that he was looking out for me—knowing that capo Charlie Stango had my back—meant that when he sent me into meetings with other mob guys in New Jersey and New York, I felt safe.

But let me be clear: not completely safe, not ever. Long experience had taught me to stay cautious and keep my head on a swivel. This was the real-life Mafia, not some TV show.

Moving between the families as I was, somebody was always testing me. Some mob guy would make a proposition to see what my reaction would be. Usually he'd be looking for a discount on price. I could have acted like any hungry street crook and made a decision behind Charlie's back, but that could have ended the operation, and maybe my life. So when I was dealing with other crews and other families, I would always respond, "All right, you know what? I gotta talk it over with my skipper. I'll see what he says. Then I'll get back to you and let you know what the price is gonna be."

Things like that almost always got back to Charlie. To ensure that they did, I sometimes used Sammy Cigars as an unwitting conduit, relating to him some incident like that. Cigars would invariably repeat the story to Gooms, and Gooms would report back to Charlie. Those little touches definitely helped cement our relationship.

24

BUILDING A CREW

WHITEY AND HIS STREET FRIENDS were constantly asking me where I was getting my product. When I started hearing that same question from members of the DeCav and Gambino families, I realized I needed to reinforce my credentials. Knowing that Jimmy Smalls had a big mouth, that he was tight with Whitey Stango and had frequent contact with Lui the Dog, I figured he would make the ideal witness to a bit of playacting. After arranging to meet with him to talk about a drug deal, I recruited one of my UC friends to call my cell phone during the meeting.

This other UC, whose undercover name was "Tamer," had a unique background. Born in the Middle East, his family had immigrated to the United States when he was still a child. He spoke perfect English, with no accent, but he was also fluent in Arabic. His bilingualism played nicely into the little performance we arranged.

To make it real, we agreed that I would let his first two calls go to voicemail and only answer on the third try. It worked perfectly.

Jimmy jumped into my car, and while we were discussing the deal my phone rang. I made a show of looking at the screen to see who it was, then pushed the call to voicemail. A couple of minutes later, the phone rang again.

Jimmy said, "Don't you want to get that?"

"Naw, not that guy. It's OK. What were you saying?"

Thirty seconds later the phone rang again. Jimmy looked at me. "Obviously the guy wants something."

"Yeah. Hold on. Let me get this."

I put the call on speaker.

"Yeah?"

"Hey, G?"

"Yeah. What's up, Tamer?"

"What's going on, buddy? What are you doing?"

"Just running around—what's up? What do you need?"

"Are you going to be around today?"

"I'm kinda tied up, man. Not today. But can I call you later?"

"Well, yeah, but you should come by. I want to see you today."

"Yeah, you know, I can try, but—"

"It's the black things. You know those brown ones I gave you last week?"

"The brown ones? Yeah."

"Well, I got black ones. I got black ones I want you to look at."

"Are you at your warehouse? Can I call you later?"

"Yeah. I—" Suddenly it sounded like he had turned away from the phone and started shouting at somebody in Arabic. He came back to me, saying, "This motherfucker! He almost dropped—!" He started screaming in Arabic again. "This fucking guy!" he says to me. "He's almost knocked a whole load over! A whole load of boxes!"

Pretending to be a calming voice, I said, "So you got the blacks now? Listen, don't say nothing. I'll come by. See you in a bit, OK?"

"All right. Make sure you do, Johnny! Don't fuck me around!"

"No, no, Tamer! Hold on to 'em. I'm coming! Don't do nothing till I get there!" And I disconnected.

By now, Jimmy was wide-eyed. "What's that about?"

"That's good, Jimmy! Really good! He's got black ones."

"Sneakers?"

"No, UGGs. Remember the brown UGGs we were selling? Now we've got them in black."

"Woo, man! We can sell those!"

"I'll call you if I need to get rid of some." I left it at that, knowing Jimmy would shoot his mouth off all over Elizabeth, solidifying my credibility.

That night, Charlie called. "Hey, what's going on, my boy?"

"Nothing much."

"You busy?"

"Nah."

"Talk to me. What are you doing?"

"Nothing much. Just running around. Might have some stuff going on in the next couple days. Might come into something."

"You mean, like, maybe something black?"

"What? Yeah, I'm working on something."

"I know you are, my boy."

"How do you know that?"

"I know everything, my boy. Don't worry about it. You just carry on."

"You're something else, Charl. You never cease to impress me. You really knew about that?"

"Come on, I know everything."

"Goddamn!"

"I'm not the captain of the ship for nothing."

When I arrived at my office the next morning, Whitey was already there, waiting for me, rubbing his hands together.

"So we got a load? We got a load of shit?"

"Nah! What are you talking about?"

"I heard we got black boots, Coz! I told everybody you got black boots! I could sell 'em!"

"They were UGGs. And I sold the whole load last night."

"I got everybody on the hook! Everybody's waiting for black boots!"

"So fucking what? What're you doing? Selling them one pair at a time? Selling them one box at a time? I sold the whole fucking load before I went to bed last night!"

"Fuck! My father said—!"

I was dismissive. "What are you going to do, set up something like a lemonade stand? What are you? A fucking *chooch*? We sell the whole load and let someone else sell them one shoe at a time! C'mon, I want to get something to eat. Want to go to lunch?"

"Yeah, all right. It's just . . . I was all excited. I thought I was gonna make a score. I thought I was—"

"Not on this one, man. It's done."

The entire act was part of my plan to always aggrandize myself—me up here, and Whitey and his punk friends down there. And it paid off in spades. A few days later, Charlie called me. "Do me a favor. Anthony needs some money. He's hurting."

"What do you want me to do?"

"He's got this job on the trucks, but he's screwing up. I'm hearing he's not showing up for work." Mickey had already told me he was having problems with Whitey. One day he'd show up, and the next day he wouldn't.

"What do you want me to do?"

"Put him under you. Take him under you. He's going to be in our crew now. He knows a lot of good kids. Just show him, take him around, do the right thing. Watch out for him; don't let him get stupid. I'm putting him under you."

I already had Mickey running around for me, and now Charlie was putting his son under me. Over time, more of Whitey's street friends would be added to the list, and I'd be building a crew. The case agents liked that. It was solidifying my position. But in the back of my mind I knew it wasn't going to be all good. Knowing Whitey, he'd be constantly begging me for a job, begging for an assignment, and begging for money. Babysitting him would eat into my quality time with his father—and cut into the already limited time I had available to spend with my real family.

In fact, Whitey's carelessness led to a situation that could have gotten me killed. He continued driving the dump truck, and one day backed into something that damaged the load bed. He called me up to ask if I knew anyone who had a welder.

"I've gotta fix this truck! Do you know anybody?"

"No, but you know what? I'm on my way to my auto body guy, the Gambino guy. I'll ask him. Where are you?"

"I'll be back at the yard soon."

"OK. Stay there and don't take the truck anywhere. I'll see what I can do."

"It can't be just any welder, Giovanni! It's gotta be an aluminum welder for the load bed."

All of that led to the incident I described at the beginning of my story, when Sammy Cigars and the Gambino guys saved me from a beating—or worse—at the hands of Luigi Oliveri and his gorillas.

25

CUGINE

By the end of 2014, my relationship with Whitey Stango was almost nonstop. He was a one-man crime spree. He had a network of underworld connections, of street gangs and random criminals of every stripe, that gave him access to guns, marijuana, and cocaine. He and I were doing a lot of business together, and we had become friends to the extent that he addressed me as "Coz" or "Cugine," from *cugino*, Italian for "cousin." He actually started introducing me to people as his cousin, and often called me in the morning after he had dropped his kids at school, asking what was planned for the day.

So now I had Whitey Stango in the morning, DeCav and Gambino eyes on me all day, and Charlie phoning me every night. When Charlie wasn't checking in with me, he was checking in with Whitey. It was getting harder and harder to get some downtime, to write my reports and be with my family.

I needed to build a story that would give me some room to breathe, and I had an idea how to do that. My plan was to give Charlie the impression that I had ongoing business deals that predated my introduction to him. In doing this, it would demonstrate that I was an earner long before I met him and justify my short absences from time to time. (As the old saying goes: "Man plans, God laughs.")

I called Charlie and said, "I'm coming out."

I gave him no specific reason; I just left it hanging. After I arrived, he and Patty joined me for breakfast at one of the cafés in the Mandalay Bay Resort and Casino. Predictably, Charlie asked me why I was there.

"I just came out to kill a couple of days."

The look on his face told me he wasn't buying it. After we'd finished eating, Charlie gave Patty twenty dollars and told her to go play the slots. She took the hint and left the table.

He confronted me. "All right! No bullshit. You ain't out here to vacation. What the fuck you doing here?"

"Nothing. Just came out to see you. Got a couple things to do. Meeting a couple of friends."

"Bullshit! What are you up to?"

I stalled in a way that signaled to him that I was being careful for his own protection. "I don't want to talk about it, Charl. Don't worry about what I'm doing. I'm just doing something. Making money."

"I know what you're doing! You're doing papanya." He leaned forward. "It's drugs?"

"I'm not talking to you about this, Charl."

"I want to know! Is it papanya?"

"Yeah, it's papanya."

"I fuckin' knew it!"

"Hold on. Hear me out. I'm not touching any of it. I'm brokering. I got a guy in Honolulu, and I got my cousin Coop and my best friend Dutch. You know, I told you about Coop and Dutch. They're bikers."

"Yeah, yeah."

"Well, my cousin, he needed a new guy, so I gave him my guy in Honolulu, and I married the two up. I came out here to do the introduction. I'm not touching any of it, Charl. I'm not going nowhere near it. I made the marriage, and I get a brokerage fee. And that's all I'm doing."

"Good. How much are we getting?"

Thank you . . .

As soon as he asked that question, I had him. Every word at our table was being recorded, and now he was on the hook for it.

"I don't know," I replied thoughtfully. "We'll see. If these guys like it, it's going to be a steady thing. Everybody's gonna . . . I'll be out here doing it a lot."

"That's good. When you go home, talk to Whitey. He's got guys with powder for you. He's got this guy 'Johnny Balls' with him. Kid knows what he is doing."

"OK, I'll talk to him."

When I got back to New Jersey, Charlie had already talked to Whitey, and the kid started right in on me, pressuring me to let him set up some coke deals. After lengthy discussions at the task force level, the case agents agreed to let me see what Whitey could do.

So I went back to him and said, "OK, listen. I talked to my guys. They want a sample. They want to see what you can do."

As it turned out, Whitey Stango's connections were very, very good. He might have sucked at everything else in life, but he was a pretty good drug dealer. He knew gang members, he knew quality, and he knew how to move product. It took him no time to set me up with a buy. As Charlie had told me, one of Whitey's key contacts was a Union City dealer whose street name was "Johnny Balls" (real name: John Capozzi).

Whitey said, "OK, listen, Cugine. Johnny won't do business with just anyone, but he knows we're together, so no problem. How much do you want? You want 200 grams? 250?"

"Make it 200."

Whitey went off to make the arrangements, but without my knowledge he ordered 250 grams. He had failed to mention that he had a guy on another crew who wanted to buy 50 grams of coke, so Whitey ordered 200 for me and an extra 50 for this other client.

We drove to an address in Union Township. When we pulled into the driveway, Whitey said, "Coz, you got to give me the money and wait here. This guy's not gonna let you in. He's real careful."

My Escalade was wired up with video and sound, so from my point of view, it was all good. I gave him the cash and he scuttled into the house. He returned a few minutes later and jumped back in the passenger seat. He had the coke in a sealed bag.

I was about to drive away, but he stopped me. "Hold on, hold on, Coz!"

"What's the matter? Let's get out of here!"

"No, no! Hold on. I gotta break off the fifty grams."

"What?"

It was only now that he admitted that he'd bought an extra fifty grams for some other guy. He pulled an extra bag out of his pocket, along with a pair of latex gloves.

I snarled at him. "What the fuck? You doing surgery right here in my car?"

"I brought a scale!" He produced a scale and set it up on the console between our seats. Then he pulled out a pocketknife. "I gotta cut this off. Do me a favor, Coz. I can't get this on my hands. I gotta drop a urine, and I can't come up hot on a piss." Whitey was on a probation order, and his PO required him to drop a urine sample once a week.

"Wait a minute! You're not doing this fuckin' operation in my car!"

"Yeah, I gotta! I got to break this off, but I can't get this shit on me. Do me a favor and cut it for me."

I didn't want to do that, as I would be contributing to the distribution of narcotics. I argued with him, "Come on, man! Not in my car!"

"No, no! Do it for me!"

"What exactly do you want me to do?"

"Just take my knife and"—he pointed—"cut off this piece right here."

My only way out of this was sabotage, so I took his knife and stabbed it into the brick of coke. The package exploded like a firecracker. Coke flew all over my car, and all over us.

"Fuck, Coz! Holy shit! Oh, my God! It's all over the car. It's all over me!"

For some stupid reason, we both started laughing—although in his case with a rising note of hysteria. Our clothes, the floor of the vehicle, and even the backseat were covered with fragments of cocaine. Whitey was visibly sweating as we scooped up as much as we could. He finally got his portion separated and weighed. He still had his gloves on, and being real cautious, he asked me to hold the main package while he put the extra fifty grams in the other bag. Then he took his gloves off.

By now I was pretty much fed up with him. I said, "Here, take your knife," and handed it back to him. Without thinking, he took it.

The knife was covered in coke, and he got it all over his hands. When he realized that, he blurted, "Oh, Coz! Oh my God, you're killing me! Oh, fuck it! Let's get out of here."

Somehow he got through his urine test, but the next Whitey-generated mishap was much more serious. It came within an inch—literally—of ending the entire undercover operation.

A week or so after the exploding coke incident, we did another deal with Johnny Balls, this time at a different house. Whitey arrived separately and met me outside. Then he went in while I waited in my car. A few minutes later, he reappeared in the driveway, beckoning at me to join him.

By exiting the vehicle, I would be leaving my surveillance team hanging. But knowing how crucial it was to maintain my role, I took a chance and got out of the car. "What's up?"

"Just come inside, come inside."

"OK, but why?"

"Just come downstairs."

I wondered, *Are these guys planning to take a shot at me?*

I was on my guard as we went into the house. The main floor was dark. We went through a narrow hallway and down a flight of stairs to a finished basement. There was a living area and a kitchen with a small island and granite countertops. Standing there was this Johnny Balls character—midthirties, thick-bodied, bald head, short beard. He had an ex-boxer look about him. As Whitey introduced me, I sensed Balls was nervous about meeting me. He was quiet, almost standoffish.

Whitey's voice filled the initial silence; he was talking real fast, all motormouthed. "Listen, Coz, we got a couple different problems. It's not all in one package. It's all zipped and air-sealed. One package is really, really, great quality, and the other one's a little weaker, but it's still good. I wanted to show you that it was good. So we're going to cook up a little bit to show you. We just want you to see that the coke is good."

"Naw, you don't have to do that."

"No, no, Johnny wants to do this! He's a straight shooter. He wants you to see this."

I didn't want any part of this. "You're not your cousin Jimmy! You're with your father, and you're with me. You're not Jimmy, so if you tell me it's good, you're not going to try to fuck me. If it's not good stuff, we'll deal with it."

But Whitey would not be dissuaded. He filled up a spoon with coke from what he had referred to as lower quality package and started cooking it up. When it was boiling, he took a copper penny, saying, "See? See the amount of oil that I'm pulling away?" And showed me the small amount of oil that had come to the top of the spoon. He scooped it up with the penny—it almost magnetized to the copper—a street method of showing the quality of the coke.

By now, all three of us were huddled over the spoon, and it took me a moment to realize that I was inadvertently smoking crack. I stepped back and tried holding my breath, but I was definitely starting to feel it.

Whitey was scheduled to drop urine again in the next couple of days. When he suddenly realized what he'd just done to himself, his reaction was almost comical. Panicking, he started breathing heavily and grabbing at his chest. "Oh, man! Oh, I think I might be having a heart attack!" Johnny and I started giggling—probably due to the intensifying effect of the crack—while Whitey continued whining. "This is serious, you guys! I think . . . oh, my heart! My heart's racing, man!"

"That's because you're a fat bastard," I kidded. "It has nothing to do with the fact that you just smoked crack."

We all ended up laughing about it. I left the basement with the drugs and returned to my vehicle. Here I was with two hundred grams of coke in my console, and although I wasn't high as a kite, I was definitely feeling the effect of those fumes. I called my backup team and, concentrating on speaking carefully, told them the deal was done and I'd meet them at an agreed location.

But as I was driving, my heartbeat was increasing. I was starting to feel more and more jacked up. On one stretch of road, as I passed a church, I got weirdly fixated on its steeple. I was gaping at this steeple, zoned out, when I realized what I was doing and looked back to check the road. Ahead was a line of cars stopped at a red light. And the last car, directly in front of me, was a police car.

I slammed on my brakes. My Escalade's tires screeched on the pavement as I slid to a halt within an inch of the patrol car. The cop looked hard at me, first in his rearview mirror and then in his sideview mirror. As he was studying me, he had the nastiest look on his face. Now I was in a huge panic, because the coke was really starting to kick in and I was dripping with sweat. If this cop got out of his car, I'd be fucked. Praying for deliverance, I looked back at him and mouthed, "I'm sorry, I'm sorry, I'm sorry." He shot me a look of disgust and shook his head. The light changed, and he kept going.

If that officer had flicked on his light bar and stepped out of his car, spotted me for being high and impaired behind the wheel, and searched my car and found the drugs, I would have been arrested. That could have ended the operation. If I wound up in lockup, then so be it. I would have kept my mouth shut, demanded a phone call to my attorney, and used the call to contact my case agents. They would have been the ones to decide whether I would break my cover.

The effects of the crack cocaine were severe enough that I had almost rear-ended that cop. I'd been lucky, but I wasn't totally out of the woods. I had told my surveillance team I'd meet them later, but obviously I couldn't show up there in my current state. As soon as the patrol car was gone and I was in the clear, I called them.

"Fuck it," I said. "I'm not driving all the way back to meet you. I'm done for the day, and I'm heading home. You guys need to come and get this coke from me. You can put it into evidence."

We agreed on a place to meet. I didn't want to explain what had happened, so when they drove up, door-to-door with me—and before they could get a good look at my sweaty face—I passed the coke across and said, "See you tomorrow. I'm outta here."

But even now my little waking nightmare wasn't over. My son had a Christmas pageant going on at preschool, and I had promised to be there. I showed up late, still wigged out, with my eyes bugging out of my head. My wife took one look at me and said, "What the hell's wrong with you? It's is the middle of winter! Why are you sweating like that? You look like you're high."

Later that evening, at home, Anna marched into our bedroom. I was lying on the bed, waiting for the crack's effects to dissipate. Her eyes drilled into me. "What's going on with you? You look stressed out or strung out. Are you using pills or something else to try to cope? If you're messed up, you should tell me, and we'll deal with it."

I came clean with her. I explained the deal I had just done and that they'd been cooking coke in front of me.

"You should go to the emergency room and get checked out," she insisted.

"Don't worry, I'm not a crackhead. I got it all under control. I just want to get good night's sleep. I've got a long day tomorrow."

Once more, I was trivializing her concerns—once more putting job before family.

26

UNWIRED

WHENEVER I WAS ON MY WAY TO A MEETING WITH A TARGET, I made it a practice to stop short of the destination and go live on my recording devices. One day, when I was scheduled to meet with Whitey at the excavation office, I called and told him I was running late. "I'll see you there after supper," I said. Whitey knew I had Johnny Balls coming to the office that evening to deliver some coke, and I'd led him to believe I'd be driving over from New York City.

I stopped at a Gulf station on Route 33. It was about ten minutes away from the office, so the location was ideal. I pulled into a darkened parking area off to one side of the station, away from the pumps.

One of my recording devices had a small lithium battery that plugged in using two tiny prongs. You had to get those two prongs into matching holes in the device. But the components were so small it was like fitting a stick up an ant's ass.

I turned on the dome light and held the device up close to my face. I normally wear reading glasses, but I didn't have them with me. In my role, it wasn't cool to wear glasses; it would make me look weak. So here I was, struggling to see what I was doing, trying to get the two prongs to line up, when the front passenger door of my Escalade suddenly flew open.

"Give me all your fuckin' money!"

When I'd heard the click of the door and spotted the black-clad figure, I had quickly bent forward, shoving the device and its dangling wires under my seat. While reaching down, I made eye contact with the intruder.

It was Whitey Stango, dressed in a long black leather coat and wearing his Yankees baseball cap turned backward. Thinking I was reaching for a gun, he immediately yelled, "Whoa, whoa, Coz! It's me! Don't shoot!"

I shouted at him, "What the fuck you doing?"

"Haw, haw! I got ya, G! I got ya! I scared the shit outta ya! You thought you were being fuckin' robbed. Whaddya doin'? Grabbing for your gun?"

"You're an idiot, bro! Get outta here, you fucking jerk! What are you doing?"

"Ah, I got Erica and some hookers in the car. We were on our way to the office and got behind ya. I said, 'Hey, there's my cugine.' I saw you pull in, so I pulled over. Thought you were making a phone call and figured I'd fuck with ya. So, we're heading over there now. What are you doing, parked here in the dark?"

"Just go to the office. I'll meet you over there."

My heart was hammering. I wasn't sure what he had seen, but if he'd walked up to the car slowly, like a real gangster and not a stupid kid, he would have seen everything. The device, the wires hanging—he definitely would have seen it. I wasn't entirely convinced that he hadn't.

I dismissed him, "Go to the fucking office!"

"Yeah, yeah. I'm going."

I knew I'd have to be extremely cautious about going to my office now. It was dark, and to get in I had to enter from behind the building, through a wooded area. I thought, *Do I continue this? How could he not have seen what I was doing?*

When I was minutes away from the office, I called him on the phone.

"Yeah?" Now a bit paranoid, my brain heard his *yeah* as being delivered in a nasty tone.

"Who's in the car with you?"

"What?"

"*Who's in the car with you?*"

"Erica. Erica's in the car with me. I told ya."

"You said you got a carload of people. Who you fuckin' bringing in the office at this time of night? Who else is with you? You know I got Johnny Balls coming!"

"No! It's just me and Erica. She just got off work. She was dancing." I knew he was banging this girl.

I said, "All right. I just wanted to make sure." So I went in the office, and everything was fine. He laughed, and I said hello to Erica. She was actually there to wrap some Christmas presents, and a few other girls—all strippers—were already in the office to wrap gifts.

The main reason we were meeting at the office that night was because Balls was scheduled to drop off some coke. After he left, Whitey put some of the packages on my desk, got out his scales, and started dividing it up, because part of the delivery had been promised to someone in his network.

Meanwhile, in a mistaken moment of Christmas spirit, I had shown Erica a couple of boxes of girls' workout shirts that were stored in my office. I told her that she and the other girls were welcome to try them on. The next thing I knew, I was surrounded by half-naked girls trying on shirts while Whitey was busy separating and packaging the coke. When he was finished, there was a layer of residue on my desk.

I blew up at him. "What are you doing, man? You got coke all over my desk! You need to clean this shit up!"

No sooner were the words out of my mouth when one of the girls piped up, "What? You're just going to throw it away? That's a lot of coke!" She grabbed a business card off my desk and started scraping the coke into a little pile. "Look! That's, like, half a gram!"

"Well, I don't want it on my desk. So get out of the way."

"Well, if you're just going to throw it away, can I have it?"

Obviously, I couldn't be encouraging anyone to do coke. I said, "Listen. I'm cleaning that up. I'm going to the bathroom to get some Windex and some paper towels. If that's stuff's gone when I get back, that's on you, sweetheart. I'm not saying you can have it. But if it's gone by the time I get back, well, I guess it's gone." I followed up, covering my ass on the recording I was making by telling her, "You shouldn't be doing that stuff, girl. It's not very healthy for you."

When I got back from the bathroom, the coke residue was gone. They had probably snorted it. I smiled forbearingly, but inside my head the real Giovanni muttered, *What a fucked-up world I'm living in. I just want to go home and see my kids.*

27

WHACK THE DOG, ACT I

BY THIS STAGE IN THE INVESTIGATION, I was traveling to Las Vegas with increasing frequency. And, at least once during each visit, Charlie would raise the subject of the DeCavs' problem child: Luigi Oliveri.

On one trip, in January 2015, I took Charlie out for dinner. While we were eating, and not for the first time, he explained all the ins and outs of the Administration to me, and how they were planning to restructure it after John Riggi died.

"Big Ears is gonna take the seat as the boss, the number one, and Milk is staying number two, the street boss, and that's how it's gonna be."

Eventually, he brought up Luigi. "The only thing is with this Luigi kid. Nobody recognizes him. This is how he's supposed to get made"— and he explained the whole procedure—"and the old man broke the rules when he did it. You understand, Giovanni?"

"Yeah, I get it. I think I understand."

"You know these guys—Big Ears, Milk—known 'em for years. They want to be the bosses, they want to be the Administration, but they don't have what it takes."

"What do you mean?"

"This Luigi, he's disrespectful. He needs to be taken care of. I talked to these guys, and they want to hurt this kid. They want to whack him out, but they were saying to me—when I was out there, in Jersey—they were saying, 'Well, we can't really do nothing. We gotta wait for a problem. He's not a big enough problem. He's gotta create real problems.' And I was telling them, 'What? You ain't got a problem? You're waiting for a problem? *Make* a fucking problem! That's what you do.'"

Charlie went on and on about it. He was like a dog with a bone. Figuring he was just blowing off steam, I played dumb and sat there, listening to him vent. "I want them to whack him out, but they won't do it!" he complained. "I said to them, 'Do him! You gotta send a message! Throw acid in his face! Run him over, put him in a wheelchair! Cripple him for the rest of his life! Fucking shoot him! Shoot him in the knees, shoot him in the balls, whatever you got to do!'"

"They really don't like this kid, huh?" I went quiet for a second, pretending to ponder. "Well, you know . . ."

"What?"

"Luigi's a good guy, but, you know, it's just a way about him. He's got a big mouth, and he's been a huge pain in my ass with his accusations and sarcastic comments. You know, those times I had him telling me I'm bad, telling me he thinks I'm a cop, telling me I'm a fucking rat, saying I'm no good. And then there's that time when he said he was going to hurt me."

"What?"

"Yeah, you know. That thing when I was over at Marco Barone's with Gooms and those guys, and you yelled at me on the phone for causing World War III. He told Gooms he was gonna hurt me. What the fuck is that?"

"What do you mean? What are you talking about?"

I laid it all out for him. The day at Barone's auto body shop when I was trying to track down an aluminum welder for Whitey. Luigi calling me, over and over, demanding that I deliver two cases of cigarettes to his social club. Luigi bragging to Gooms about him and his gorillas planning to drag me into the basement of his club to answer questions.

At that moment, it was like a lightbulb went on in Charlie's head. "Hah! Well, maybe . . . yeah! Maybe *you're* the problem!"

I asked myself, *What? How am I the problem?*

Charlie answered that thought. "*You* could be the problem! You know what, Giovanni? You should fucking do this kid. That's what we should do. He's never gonna go away, so you make him go away. That's what's gotta happen." He paused, and then he said the words. "He's gotta meet death."

Now I was thinking, *Smart move. Now you've really put your foot in it.*

Murder for hire, entrapment issues—because of all the legal aspects, I had to be extremely careful about what I said next. On the other hand, Charlie was the one pushing for violent action.

"I have to say," I ventured, with a grin, "I'd love to meet Luigi in a dark alley sometime. See how much of a tough guy he really is without his crew. Or maybe I should tell Coop and Dutch what he's been saying about me and then introduce him to them."

Charlie's eyes widened. "That's it, Giovanni! You should introduce him to those guys!"

"No way, Charl! That would not play out well for Luigi."

"That's what I mean! Get those guys to help you get at Luigi. Would they help you?"

"Sure. They would do anything for me."

"Would they do something with you like maiming or killing this little fuck?"

"Not a doubt in my mind. They're both capable guys." By saying that, I indicated that I had direct knowledge of them having murdered or attempted to murder in the past.

"That's it! You should get hold of those guys. Feel 'em out. See if they'll help you."

It was a revealing conversation, all nicely recorded, but it was time to put the brakes on.

"Aw, Charl, that's not for me to decide. I don't decide these things. That's your thing, your department."

"I'm going to run it up the chain, talk to the Administration." He couldn't have looked more satisfied.

Within days, he came back to me, saying he'd spoken with the Administration. "I explained to them that now we do have a problem. They agreed it needs to be taken care of. They said, 'Put him in the river.' You need to step up here, Giovanni. You can't let people walk on you like this. People like this, you gotta meet head-on. You gotta be the man you were born to be, you understand."

"Well, you know, I'm just saying . . . it's a big step."

"Yeah, it's a big step."

"I don't know . . . a guy like me, Charl? I'm a nobody."

"You're not a nobody!"

"If I did this, and I took this guy's life, don't you think everybody's gonna come at me?"

"What're you talking about?"

"Even though they're fed up with him, he's still a made guy. As Lui told me himself, I'm just a fuckin' civilian."

"You ain't no civilian!"

"In your eyes, I'm not. And I appreciate that, I do, but in the *borgata*'s eyes, I'm a civilian, right?"

"No fucking way! You're with me!"

"I'm just saying, where does that leave me? People are going to come at me. People are going to want revenge."

He snorted a laugh. "They'll be standing fifty fucking deep waiting to pin medals on your chest! What do you mean, you're a nobody? You want to be a somebody, I'll make you a somebody! Listen to me. You and me, right? You speak for me! You gotta do what I would do! You got to be the man you were born to be. Understand?" Charlie's ice-blue eyes narrowed, and he looked at me as if the world had stopped. "You got a problem with what we're asking you to do here, Giovanni?"

Knowing my ass was on the line, I quickly shot back, "Naw, naw. Don't think I haven't got it in me. But, you know, it's just concerns I have. I'm not an official fucking member."

"Well, that's what makes you! That's what pushes you up! Trust me, my boy."

"You're my captain, my skipper, I'll do whatever you see fit, Charl. We're in it together, right?"

"Yeah, man! This is going to be a beautiful thing! This is going to be great!"

After that, Charlie wouldn't stop talking about it all through the rest of the meal and all through the drive back to Henderson. "This is good shit! This is fucking . . . *aaah!*" He wanted Luigi dead, and he wanted me to make it happen.

Along the way, he upped the ante: "As a matter of fact, the Administration says if we're going to kill him, we should probably take out his captain, too, Manny Riggi. They don't want any beefs once the old man is gone. The old man's going to die off soon."

After that conversation, and those recordings, I figured I was done. I expected that as soon as I completed my debrief with the team back in New Jersey, my undercover operation would be shut down.

After I got home, the FBI immediately applied under Title III and got a wiretap order so they could listen to all of Charlie's conversations. If he was going to be discussing these murders with the incoming Administration, they wanted to hear it. In the meantime, although everyone knew the operation might swiftly come to an end, I was given authorization to carry on. The instruction was simple: "Take it as far as you can."

So I did.

Just before I left Las Vegas on that pivotal trip, Charlie had said, "Do me a favor. When you get back, go see my goombah, Joey Collina. Joey's a captain like me. He's fallen on some hard times. See if you can help him out. Maybe you could do some stuff for him. Get him a little money. He's held down, he's on a bracelet . . . finishing up a sentence. But he's in bad health, so he could use some cash. He's got a crew with some things going on. Maybe we can help each other out."

"Sure. You want me to drop some money off to him?"

"Yeah, yeah. If you're doing anything with that auto parts guy, the one that's with Uncle Joey, and you make any money, break him off a little something, and tell him it's from me."

Whitey happened to know this "auto parts guy" his father had mentioned. His name was Eddie, and he ran an auto supply business. We paid him a visit.

"Listen, your skipper Joey . . . are you taking care of him on your end?"

"Don't worry. Whatever I do, I always take care of Joey. I always kick up to him."

That was fine, and good to know, but from an investigative standpoint, I wanted to close the loop between Charlie and Uncle Joey by getting a meeting with the old man. I couldn't just assume from a conversation with Eddie that Uncle Joey was in fact getting his kick-up. I wanted to personally drop off some money to him, so I told Charlie that I didn't trust anybody to pay someone like Uncle Joey on our behalf. I suggested that I do it as Charlie's representative and deliver any personal messages at the same time.

Charlie agreed. He instructed me, "Take whatever cut is owed to Uncle Joey, and you and Whitey drop it off. Tell him this is from his goombah Charlie. Tell him I miss him and I'll see him soon."

I explained to Whitey that we'd be paying Uncle Joey a visit. He didn't get it. "All right, you want me to just swing by for you? He lives right by me. I can drop off some cash."

"No! Listen to me! I've got a message for him from your father. I speak for your father, so I'm going to do this myself. Call Uncle Joey and tell him we're stopping by."

It probably looked a bit strange to Whitey that I was insisting on a meeting with this capo at his home. In the real world, I would have said, "Sure. Here's five hundred—take it to Uncle Joey." But I took this position with Whitey for two reasons: first, to keep him on a short leash, and second, I wanted the money to come directly from me.

While this little dance was going on, we'd been hearing that Jimmy Smalls had been arrested, and not just once. As soon as he'd made bail on the domestic violence case, he was picked up again on firearms and drug charges. Then, unaccountably, he was released on bail again. Knowledgeable residents of the neighborhood couldn't figure it out, and some were wondering if Smalls had become an informant or made some kind of deal. Coincidentally, and unknown to us, he had also recently cheated Eddie out of $20,000.

When Whitey and I walked into the Uncle Joey's house, the first thing he did was study me through oversized, thick-lensed glasses and say, "Giovanni? Wow, you look familiar! Do we know each other? We never met? You look so familiar."

I pretended to study this old guy's face as he ambled toward me, wheeling an oxygen tank. He was in his early seventies, with the stereotypical raspy voice of an old-time gangster. "Naw," I said. "Don't recognize you."

In fact, a few years earlier I had been peripherally involved in a roundup of some organized crime guys, and Joey had been arrested in that sweep. I wasn't sure, but I thought I might have been part of the team that locked him up. All I could do was brush it off. "Naw."

"No? You look so familiar!"

"Nope."

That was it. "All right. Come in. Sit down."

So we sat down, and I passed him some cash, compliments of Charlie. Everything went well. But when Whitey and I started to tell him a few things about what we had going on, he held up a hand. "Let's go to the basement and talk where it's quiet." In other words, where the feds might not have planted a bug.

Downstairs, he opened up a bit about the family and the Administration. At one point in the conversation, Whitey mentioned Jimmy Smalls. "You know Jimmy's out on bail, right?"

"What?"

"Yeah, and you know who he's with now? He's with the Dog. You know, the Pet."

It took a moment to jog his memory. "The Pet? Oh, Luigi! Luigi Oliveri."

"Yeah."

"That Luigi's a nobody, a fucking nobody! Somebody better tell that guy he better not stick his fucking nose in my business!" He turned to me. "Listen, Giovanni, this Luigi isn't what he thinks he is. He's not a made guy. He's not a serious guy. Things are going to change. When I'm done, and your father's done"—referring to Charlie Stango as if he were my father—"things are going to change." He snorted in disgust. "But for now, we got to let it be."

He swung his attention back to Whitey. "And that cousin of yours . . . Jimmy? I'm going to hurt him bad. He's going to the hospital. He beat Eddie outta twenty grand. I told your father, and he said, 'Hey, do what you gotta do.' I don't want to kill the kid, because he's your father's nephew, but he's going to the hospital. If he's down here near me, and you know he's down in my area, you better let me know. You better call me! I'll leave the fucking house to take care of him myself!"

As we were leaving, he said, "All right, you guys . . . when you leave, be careful out there. Watch for the cops. Don't get arrested. Be safe, and don't wind up like me."

It will come as no surprise that my repeated trips to Las Vegas weren't making life any easier on the home front. Each time, as soon as I arrived in Vegas, it was a logistical nightmare.

On one occasion, I called Anna from the hotel phone. "I saw you texted me five, six times, called me three times, but I haven't had my phone. How is everything at home? How are you and the kids?"

"Why? Where is it? Where's your phone?" she demanded.

"C'mon, you know I can't always call you when I'm working."

To Anna, that sounded like a lie. She might have done undercover work, but she'd never worked deep cover. All she knew was that I was spending a lot of time in Las Vegas, and that particular city's reputation for debauchery had her imagination working overtime. She was beginning to suspect that, to convince the mob guys of my bona fides, I was probably partying all night and sleeping with other women. Such suspicions did nothing to improve our home situation, and the final months of the operation brought us close to divorce.

As I readily and gratefully admit today, if it wasn't for Anna's strength, devotion, and iron determination, our marriage would never have survived.

28

CONTROLLING
THE CRAZIES

BACK AT THE EXCAVATION COMPANY, it was business as usual—meaning "unusual." In addition to our own supply of counterfeit goods, I was sometimes buying and selling swag that had been hijacked in the street. Parallel to this, I was continuing to do drug deals with Johnny Balls. I knew Whitey was probably keeping his father up to date on those deals, so I pointedly refrained from saying anything about them to Charlie. It looked better that way. He would think I was trying to protect him. Despite this pretense, on one of my trips to Vegas, he let slip how much he actually knew.

"That kid Johnny Balls, he's a stand-up kid. He's got good stuff."

"OK . . . So now you know I took your advice about the coke."

He did, and by the end of the conversation, it was clear he was giving me his blessing to put Johnny Balls in my crew. So now I effectively had Mickey, the excavation company owner, Whitey, and now this guy Johnny Balls. Balls had his own thing going and was fairly independent, but he soon made it clear he was at my beck and call if I needed something.

That doesn't mean I would ever have any respect for the guy. On one occasion, Balls dropped off some coke at my office while he was on his way to Atlantic City with his preteen daughter and her friends.

He told me the kids were involved in a pep rally or some kind of cheer-leading event. By now I was pretty much hardened to the amorality of the criminal world, but I couldn't believe this jerk was so low that he would transport a load of coke in a car full of ten-year-old girls. Those kids were about the same age as my own daughter. The whole episode sickened me.

Next, wouldn't you know it, Whitey decided to do some recruiting of his own. He brought in a kid named Mario Galli—a heavyset, twentysomething street thug. He mentioned him to me one night at the office, saying, "Hey, Giovanni, we could really use Mario. He's a solid guy. He'd be good for us."

Playing the gangster role, I replied laconically, "Bring him around. I'll meet him."

When I met Mario, the first thing I noticed was that he and Whitey looked like bookends, both big guys, both overweight. Whitey started right in, pitching for him: "He'll do anything we need. I was thinking of using him on a couple of things."

"Yeah? What can he do?"

Mario answered for himself. "Well, I got marijuana, I got access to a lot of stuff. Whatever you need, I'll be there."

So I said, "OK. Let's see what you can do. We'll see where it goes."

The three of us left the office and went for a meal. In that brief time, Whitey must have decided that he'd moved up the pecking order and that he was now a full-fledged crew boss himself. When we left the restaurant, he started ordering Mario around. He handed the kid his keys. "Go start the car."

Mario did as he was told. He started Whitey's car and then sat in it, waiting.

I said, "I'll call you tomorrow."

Whitey went through the double-kiss performance, right there on the street. "All right, Cugine. All right."

"Tell Mario I'll see him later."

Whitey banged on the hood of his car. "Hey! Get the fuck out of the car! Come say good-bye! What are you doing? This man just gave you his time!" *This man*—he was talking about me.

Mario jumped out of the car, looking flustered, and gave me the two kisses.

"Yeah, yeah, nice to meet you, kid."

Replaying that little scene later, I couldn't help but laugh. At some level, Whitey had been imitating his father—going on the record for Mario, *with me*. And the Giovanni Gatto in me had been perfectly happy to play the role of a scary crew boss.

And so, in the course of just a few weeks, and mostly due to Charlie's influence, my crew had expanded to include a drug dealer and some street muscle. The trouble was that now I had to spend more and more of my precious time trying to save these idiots from themselves.

On one occasion, not long after Mario joined the crew, I went along with Whitey to see Eddie, the guy with the auto supply store. He and Whitey had come up with a plan to rob a warehouse.

Eddie said, "It's a huge load—a $1.2 million load. We can hijack the whole thing. We can take the guard and wrap him up in duct tape. Tape him to the chair."

Whitey added to this lunacy. "Yeah, Coz! We can get one of them sippy juice boxes the kids use for their school lunches, tape it to his chest, and put the straw in his mouth. If the guard dies in the chair, we could use the juice box as a defense." The pair of them sat there in front of me, dead serious, laying out this deranged plan.

I listened, and then I said, "All right, let me play it back for you guys. You want to pistol-whip an old guy, the guard at this warehouse. You want to tie him to a chair, duct tape some kind of juice box to his chest so he can drink from it while he sits there bleeding and you're emptying the warehouse into a truck. And you guys think that's a smart fucking idea?"

"Well, what else are we gonna do? We need to make a score."

"Well, what are your other options?"

Eddie piped up. "What about if we take down a truck? Force it over to the side of the road, pistol-whip the driver, split his fucking skull open, and take his load. That's probably the easiest."

"All right . . . maybe. Let me think about it."

As an undercover, if I was going to get involved with this, I'd have to get these two masterminds to come out one night, let them scope out the area and talk up their plan, get it all on tape, and then have the team take them down for conspiracy. It would be a great charge, but, logistically, with all the things the task force had going on, none of our case agents would want to cover that. We were running an LCN operation, and the Bureau was in it for bigger fish than these two lowlifes. So, to buy time, I said, "Hold on, hold on! Let me see, let me think about it."

Whitey came back to me soon after. "What do you think, Coz? Let's do this! Grab some guns and do this."

"Hold the fuck on! I want to do that, but I have another load coming in. It's sure money." I came up with another imaginary truckload of swag that I had a line on. I used that to put him off a few times. Another time, I said to him, "I'm making money on another deal. I don't want to talk about it right now."

"Well, you know, it's a big load!"

"You're not thinking right. You're thinking big load . . . and if you get caught, it's big time. You've got to think smaller right now." That's how I tried to control him, but his desperation for money was a constant problem.

For recording purposes, I would sometimes arrange a meeting in my office at the excavation company, or occasionally take everyone out for lunch or dinner to discuss the things everyone had going on. The more time I spent around these guys, the more it became clear that they were willing to commit just about any criminal act to prove themselves to me and Charlie. I realized that the only way to keep them in line was to start acting like a hard-assed crew boss. I told them they had to fill me in on anything they were thinking about or planning, so as not to step on any other *borgata*'s toes.

They seemed receptive to my demands, but I wasn't completely sure I'd gotten through to them. But then a textbook opportunity presented itself.

We had all gone for lunch at an Italian restaurant in Carteret, New Jersey, after meeting with some Colombo guys about a potential alliance in the shipping business. Five of my still-expanding crew were with me, including Mickey, Whitey, and Mario. My recorders were on, and I was just sitting quietly, letting them talk.

Mickey started warning them that we all had to be careful about RICO. "We all gotta watch for this RICO," he explained. "We could all get fucked up and go down. RICO hits you and you're dead!" The rest of the crew were all nodding in agreement.

Of course, I knew the RICO they were talking about—the federal law entitled the Racketeer Influenced and Corrupt Organizations Act, colloquially known as the RICO Act. The trained undercover within me realized that this was a perfect opening—a chance to demonstrate both street-criminal ignorance and strong leadership in one performance.

Pretending to become visibly upset, I interjected, "What the hell are you talking about? Who the fuck is this guy Rico, and why are you all talking like you're afraid of him?"

As they all looked at each other, confused as to why I looked so pissed off and disappointed. Mickey stepped in and tried to explain it to me in a calm and guarded way. "No, Giovanni . . . we're talking about RICO!"

"I heard what you said, Mick! But I don't know who he is and why you're so afraid of someone. We take care of our business, and we should not fear anyone!"

Treading lightly, Mickey continued. "Giovanni . . . RICO is the federal racketeering charge that could put us all in prison."

I played stupid and demanded an explanation. They all looked at me just as I wanted them to: as a dangerous but uneducated street animal who had no understanding of federal laws because he didn't care to know about them.

Mickey broke it down for me in detail, using our own organization as an example. "Giovanni," he concluded, "the RICO statute is a federal charge that could put us all away. Everything we are doing and saying could be tied to you and then all the way up to Charlie . . . all the way out in Vegas. It shows that we are a criminal enterprise."

As I listened to Mickey's accurate explanation of the federal violation, I pretended to become very concerned for the well-being of all of us. I scanned their faces. "Really? That's fucked up, that the bulls can just put that kind of shit on us. So, listen up, all of you! Charlie can't afford that kind of time." I focused my gaze on Whitey. "Anthony, we all really gotta be careful for your daddy's sake. He ain't going back inside because of someone's stupidity. You all need to be real careful! From now on, I want each of you to tell me everything you've got going on. And make sure you don't do anything behind my and Charlie's back!"

Wide eyes and nodding heads signaled that I had driven the point home.

Sometimes as an undercover you can't plan for moments like that. They just fall into your lap. The whole time this exchange was going on, I was thinking, *Man, I hope this whole conversation comes up clear on the tape so it can be played for a jury one day!*

———————

Of course, it wasn't long before Whitey came up with another brilliant idea on how to make money. He and Mario would start an escort service.

"We got girls! We got strippers! We can do this!"

I tried to blow them off, but then I got a call from Charlie: "Anthony's talking about doing something with girls. Maybe look into it for me."

I couldn't be involved in this. Cops can't be running prostitution rings; I couldn't be a pimp. Charlie wanted me to meet with Whitey and Mario and get the details so he could run it up the chain. I had to find a way around it, so when Whitey told me that he and Mario were meeting three of the girls at a restaurant in Toms River, I decided to join them. I made it look like I was just stopping by to have a drink and meet everybody—not to talk business, just to hang out for a few minutes. As soon as I sat down, Whitey introduced me to a trio of mascaraed, well-endowed young women, all of whom certainly looked the part.

He launched right into it. "Hey, Cugine. What we're thinking about doing is . . . Gina here used to be a dancer, and she used to run this thing on the side. She was like a madam, and she's pretty good at it."

"You don't need to tell me all this."

"Well, I want you to know. I want to do this thing."

"Well, that's on you."

He replied with these words: "I want to put it on the record. I want to put this on the record that we're going to do this."

"You want to put it on the record with who? With me? You want to go on the record with *me* with this thing? Listen, do I really need to tell you—?"

But he just kept on talking, laying it all out. Mario would be the driver, Whitey would be the girls' protection, the client would pay a certain amount and, as he put it, "Whatever the girls make on the side getting banged is all separate money."

I decided the best thing for me to do was sit back and listen. That way, if it ever became necessary, the recording I was making could be used in evidence. When he'd finished sketching out their plans, I said, "OK, listen to me. I don't need to know each and every detail of what you're doing. You girls won't be working for me, and whatever you decide to do as a group right here, that's for you. If you girls choose to do this with Whitey, that's for you and him to work out." I pointed at Whitey. "From you, all I'll need to hear is how much money you're sending to your father. That's all I care about, because that's all he cares about. All the other details . . . you're a big boy, so you work it out. You don't need me to tell you how to do this."

I turned to Gina, the woman who was going to be the madam. "You say you've done this before?"

She nodded.

"Then you're good. Everybody understand?"

One of the servers stopped by the table and asked me, "Are you going to have something to eat? You got here late. Would you like to order some food?"

"No, sweetheart. I gotta go. But do me a favor, would you? Give me the bill." She brought it to me. I looked at it, and threw $200 on the table. "Here you go, guys. That'll cover your dinner."

When I stood up to leave, each of the girls got up and gave me a kiss good-bye. Then Anthony and Mario each went through the ritual kiss performance, and the pair of them walked me out.

On the way to my car, Whitey tried to hit me up for some money. "Hey, Coz, you got a couple hundred extra? I need a couple hundred to get me by."

I wheeled on him. "What the fuck? I just paid for your dinner! What did we just talk about? Go out and earn some money. I'm not giving you nothing. I'm not running a day care here."

He marched back into the restaurant, looking totally pissed off. I wasn't worried about his disappointment at my reaction. I knew that if his father had been standing there, he would have approved.

The whole encounter was an exasperating waste of my time, but if Whitey and Mario ever did get their project up and running (they didn't), at least I had all of their plans on tape.

29

WHACK THE DOG, ACT II

CHARLIE NEVER STOPPED TALKING ABOUT THE HIT ON LUIGI. To keep him happy, I decided it was time to introduce him to my potential shooters.

My "Cousin Coop," and my "Buddy Dutch," were supposedly two longtime biker friends of mine. Both men were seasoned undercover operators, and, in fact, we were all close friends in real life. Charlie had already suggested that I should hire them to whack out the Dog, and they fit the role perfectly—shaven heads, beards, tattoos, the whole act. Charlie already believed that I was brokering drug deals using these guys, so I arranged for the two of them to show up during one of my Las Vegas visits. The idea was to provide an opportunity for Charlie to meet the prospective hit men and see how easily I interacted with them.*

Charlie and I met for breakfast at Raffles, a restaurant (since renamed) in the Mandalay Bay Hotel. I had already told him that Coop and Dutch were in town and staying in the hotel. The setup was for a "chance meeting" in Raffles. By prearrangement, the bikers were sitting around a corner, just out of sight.

---

* That part of the performance wasn't going to be a problem: I love these two guys, genuinely and wholeheartedly, and they love me back. When we do something together, the connection is obvious, because we're not faking it.

While we were eating, a waitress came over. She was carrying a drink—a Bloody Caesar. She set it on the table.

"What's this?" I asked.

"This is from Dutch and Coop."

"What? You're kidding me." I started laughing. "Ah, OK." I made a show of looking past her. "Are they here?"

"Yeah, they're right around the corner."

I said to Charlie, "Excuse me one minute," and got up and went to the corner. I saw them sitting there, and said, "Thank you."

Loud laughter, so that Charlie would hear it.

Returning to our table, I told him, "The guys are just making fun of me, because this Caesar is my cure-all for a hangover. We had a lot to drink last night."

When we finished our meal, I said, "You want to come and say hello?"

"Yeah, why not?"

"Better come now. I don't know what these animals are going to do later. They can go off on a tear, get on a couple of bikes, and I won't see them for days. That's how they live."

"Yeah, yeah. I knew those guys. I was inside with a lot of them. I get it. It's your cousin. Let's go say hello."

We headed for the corner, but as soon as Charlie laid eyes on the two bruisers, all beards and muscles and tattoos, his sneakers skidded to a halt on the polished floor. He put a hand in front of me. "Whoa, whoa, no fucking way. Nah, nah, nah! Giovanni, I can't. I can't go over there."

"What do you mean, Charl? C'mon."

"Naw, naw, Giovanni. It's not—it's no good. You know what? Tell 'em I said hello, tell 'em I'll see you maybe later for a drink or something. We'll do this later."

"What's the matter? That's my cousin, Coop. That's my best friend, Dutch. Like brothers to me. They're like my family."

"I know they're your family, but you know. . . . All right. Real quick, real quick!"

So, only out of respect for me, he accompanied me over to their table. I said, "Dutch, Coop, this is Charlie. This is my dear friend, Charlie."

They both stood up, and they couldn't have been more cordial. "How are you, sir? Pleased to meet you." They were well spoken, but they had that little bit of stink on them. Dutch said, "So good to meet you, Charlie. Giovanni here says you're a great guy. Real nice to meet you."

"Yeah, yeah. You guys enjoy your breakfast, right. I just wanted to say hello, and I gotta go."

The whole thing took twenty seconds, tops, and Charlie beat a retreat. I walked him out. "Charl, thanks. Means a lot to me, 'cause this is the only family that I got."

"Yeah. But let me go, Giovanni. I gotta run."

I went back inside and sat down with the boys. They both looked mortified.

"Man, that sucks!" Coop said. "That kind of went shitty."

"No," I said. "It was beautiful. Fucking priceless."

They were both saying, "Are you kidding?"

"Guys, you don't understand. You didn't act like thugs. You didn't step over the line. You didn't play outlaw bikers. You were just two big, solid guys. You were just what I needed you to be. You have no idea what you did for me just now." And, really, it could not have been scripted better, because sometimes too long is too much. Sometimes quicker is more.

When I got back to my room, Charlie called. "Giovanni! Them guys! Yeah, fuckin' dynamite guys. Solid guys, but Johnnie, you can't have them guys at that hotel!"

"What do you mean?"

"Naw, naw. You're all staying at the same fucking hotel? You can't do that. I get it that you're friends. I get it, it's your cousin. I understand that, but you can't be in the same place as them. You see them guys? They're not us. They don't look like us. We don't blend. You're bringing too much attention to yourself. You can't have them there. You gotta put them in another hotel. Take them and put them down on Fremont Street." In other words, *Put them where the shit people stay in Las Vegas. They belong downtown, away from the Strip.*

"I don't mind if you meet them for a drink or whatever, but that's what I think. Too many eyes in the sky watching us, Giovanni.

Everybody's on video. We got the Metro out here, we got the FBI out here, we got state and local cops out here. You gotta assume, when you're out here, we're always being watched."

"All right, Charl. I'll do that. I didn't mean, you know . . . I wasn't thinking." Again, I had to play dumb, because this was supposedly a new world to me, and I had to let him "teach" me.

Which was fine, because I ended up with another really good recording.

———————————

Through all of this, and during these multiple trips to Las Vegas, my personal relationship with Charlie continued to blossom. And in many ways, his live-in girlfriend played an unwitting role in that growing trust.

The first couple of times I visited their home in Henderson, Charlie would be waiting for me in his driveway. But before long, I was just pulling up and walking into the house. I'd call and say, "Hey, I'm leaving the Strip. I'll be there in twenty minutes." I'd park in the driveway, walk through the garage, and go straight into the kitchen.

If I needed to use the bathroom and Charlie or Patty was using the one on the main floor, I could just walk upstairs, right through the master bedroom, and use their en suite. I basically had run of the house, and a lot of that had to do with my relationship with Patty.

As time went on, she had begun joining us for lunches and dinners, and she often invited me over to the house for breakfast. She'd get on the phone to me at my hotel. "Don't eat breakfast! Come here for breakfast." She knew I liked hot sauce on my eggs, she knew I liked ciabatta bread, she knew how I liked my coffee, and she went out of her way to make me happy. She'd put a bottle of water on the table for me and sit there while I was eating. Even more, when Charlie was upstairs changing clothes, she didn't hesitate to unburden herself, often complaining to me about his nephew Jimmy or his son Whitey.

"Anthony's a drain on his father, Giovanni. He's no good. He's a piece of shit. He married that whore, that stripper . . ." and on and on.

Once in a while, she would bring up Lena, my fictional girlfriend, talking about her as if she knew her. She even felt entitled to break my horns. "Look at you, Giovanni. You're all gashed up. Does Lena know you were out last night?"

I played the part. "Naw, Patty . . . don't say nothing. If Lena comes out here, if you ever meet her, don't tell her I've been running around."

I have no problem admitting that Patty was starting to grow on me. Her hospitality and caring ways, making my coffee the way I liked it, making my stays in Vegas more comfortable, giving me hugs, and joking around—it all took on a familiar and comfortable feel, and I found myself looking forward to seeing her. I came to understand that I was helping to fill a void in her life. What Patty had always wanted with Charlie was a relationship with both him and his children, a sense of a family unit. She'd never had that because Whitey was a one-man domestic train wreck, always screwing up, and Charlie's law-abiding eldest son kept his father and Patty mostly at arm's length. All she got for her efforts toward domestic harmony were headaches and heartaches.

Patty's intensifying warmth toward me also had a marked influence on my relationship with Charlie. I think that's when he really fell in love with me. More than once he said, "Listen, Giovanni. You don't have to stay in hotels when you're out here. You know that, right? Our house is your house."

For me, staying as a guest in their home was never going to work. So whenever he brought that up, I would respond with "I know, I know. I appreciate it, Charl. But no, I don't want to do that. I don't want to disturb you guys."

"Well, listen, we've got that extra bedroom. It's there for you. I just want you to know that. Patty says you don't have to stay in hotels. She wants you to stay with us. I told her you probably don't want to stay here because you want to be partying, getting drunk with your buddies."

That was always my out. "Yeah, Charl. I really do appreciate the offer, but you're right. It's my time to blow off fuckin' steam when I'm out here."

There was a little fireplace in their dining area, and its mantel was lined with pictures—a photo of Charlie's mother, a few of his grandkids, and, off to the right, a picture of an Italian guy with a moustache sitting by a window smoking a big cigar.

The first time I noticed the photos, I said, "Cute pictures of the kids, there. That's Anthony's son, right?"

"Yeah. And that's my mother over there. That's my granddaughter, that's my grandsons, and that there"—he pointed proudly—"that's JoJo Ferrara. That's *my* guy, Giovanni. He was my skipper. That man made me what I am." He talked more about JoJo Ferrara than he did anybody else on that mantelshelf. "He's gone now. Passed away." He was grinning. "Man, I did things for that man!" I immediately associated that remark with murders he'd committed. "Yeah, me and Tango, Ray Tango, we ran around. JoJo would tell us to do something and we'd do it. Drop of the hat, we'd do it!"

"Yeah? Ray Tango?"

"Are you kidding? We did everything! In the street, that's why they called me Charlie the Hat! I'd turn my hat around . . . and everybody knew shit was going to happen."

I had already heard the lore. If Charlie removed his hat, or turned it around on his head, when he was out on the street, people started running, because it meant somebody was going get beaten half to death or die. "It's on! It's on!" was one of his sayings. He told me, "Me 'n' Ray Tango . . . I think we killed more people by mistake . . . by accident. But we were some team, my boy, and I ain't kidding." He told me that Ray Tango was still in lockup, but he was getting out. "And when he does, it's going to be a good thing for us!"

30

MOBSTER CONCLAVE

EVERY TIME I FLEW OUT TO LAS VEGAS, I would stay on the Strip. I tried to move around and not stay in the same hotel every time. I didn't want my face to become too familiar to hotel staff, so over the months, I alternated between the ARIA, the Vdara, the Mandalay Bay, the Bellagio, and a few others.

Charlie loved the Strip, so he'd make it a point to see me at wherever I was staying, and we'd have a meal together. Occasionally, he would make his own way to my hotel, but most of the time I had to drive out to Henderson and pick him up. On each visit, I would rent a sharp looking car that I knew the old-school capo would like—usually a Cadillac.

During my next visit after his encounter with Dutch and Coop, Charlie and I were scheduled to meet a "tour group" of members and associates from the Lucchese and the Genovese crime families. Charlie was all pumped up about getting together with these guys, and of course, my case agents were keen for me to nail some good recordings.

Charlie hadn't said exactly what time we were going to meet these guys. He told me he'd let me know. I was really craving a bit of alone time, so I took a chance and went for a sightseeing drive outside the city. It was probably about eighty degrees when I left the Strip, but as I climbed through various canyons and along mountainsides, the air temperature dropped. After about forty minutes of winding roads, I found myself at the bottom of a ski hill in a place called Lee Canyon.

This close to Las Vegas, and people were skiing? I thought that was kind of unique, so I drove around, took a few pictures, and just used the time to mentally recharge.

So there I was, eight thousand feet up a mountain road, fifty miles from Las Vegas, when my cell rang. It was Charlie, calling for his ride.

"Where are ya?"

"On the Strip," I lied. "Having something to eat."

"Come get me. We gotta meet these guys. They're waiting for us."

Now I faced a huge problem. I had to race back to the Strip, stop at my hotel, change my clothes, grab my recorders from my cover team, and haul ass out to Henderson. I shot down off that mountain, but as I was working my way through the outskirts of the city, I realized I was running low on gas. Cursing, I stopped at the next station.

When I got out to fill the tank, I discovered that my car was no longer the shiny black mobster-impressing Caddie I had rented. It was covered in red dust from the roads I'd been traveling. It looked like I'd been four-wheeling out in the desert.

I ran into the station to ask directions to the nearest car wash.

"It's Sunday," the cashier told me. "Most of them are closed on Sundays."

"What? What are you talking about? You being funny?"

"No. It's Nevada—a lot of Mormons. A lot of stuff is closed on Sunday."

Now I was in full panic mode. "You got a hose?" There was a mechanic's bay next to the gas station. "You got a hose in the garage? I really need to wash my car off!"

"I don't have access to that."

"Where's the nearest gas station other than you?"

"There's one about a half-mile . . ." She gave me directions.

I said, "Do me a favor. Can you call them up? I'm in a real big hurry, and I need to get my car cleaned. I've gotta have a clean car!"

She helped me out and made the call, saying to whoever answered, "I've got somebody here who needs his car cleaned. You guys have a hose he could use real quick?" She said to me, "Yeah, they have a hose you can use."

I thanked her, paid for my gas, drove down to the next station, and hosed my car off as best I could.

Meanwhile, Charlie was blowing up my phone. "Where the fuck are you?"

"Charl, listen, give me time. I got in my car, and then I got a flat. I had to turn around, find a gas station. I'm getting there, I'm getting there."

"Jesus Christ! OK, but hurry the fuck up!"

It seemed like every five minutes he was calling me. "On your way yet?"

"Naw. I'm having a problem. I'm—"

"Forget about it! I'll drive myself over there."

I couldn't allow that. I didn't want to miss recording a good conversation with him on the way there, and with these other guys when we arrived. He had all these New York mobsters waiting for him—prominent organized crime figures and associates—and I didn't want to miss any of that.

"No, no! I'm coming, I'm coming, Charl! Just give me ten minutes. I'll be there, I'll be there."

"Jesus Christ!"

In a strange way, this delay and general screw-up worked out, because I needed to be sloppy sometimes. The sloppiness made my criminal persona a bit more authentic. It kind of worked out in the end. But in the middle of it, when I was living it, trying to juggle all this stuff, calling my cover agent and telling him, "I've got to swing by! Come downstairs! I need the recorders! I've got to run!" it ate at my insides.

I got the recording devices and ran out to Henderson. That drive was tough on the nerves as well, because as much as I wanted to put my foot down, I couldn't get caught speeding. I was in the middle of Nevada, and if I got pulled over by a cop I'd end up on the locals' radar. Even a speeding ticket issued to my false identity could become an administrative nightmare. I'd had one once before, during a different undercover operation, and was just a huge pain in the ass.

The whole experience was agonizing, but I got there and picked up Charlie, and everything was fine.

While we were driving into the city, Charlie circled back to the subject of Luigi. He gave me the final go-ahead to use Coop and

Dutch. "Yeah, you should use those guys. Get your friends to do it with you."

"OK. It's in the works. It's coming along."

But he kept on about it, pressuring me, so to slow it down, I told him that Dutch had another shooter—a solid guy that he trusted, a guy who had done it before. "I don't know who he is, Charl, but if Dutch tells me he's good, he's good. But the problem is, this other guy . . . he's on paper. He's going to be off parole in a couple of months. I don't know when." I was saying whatever I could to buy time. I didn't want to have to go back to New Jersey and tell everybody, *He's leaning on me. He wants me to kill this guy right now.* If I did, the FBI would take the case down.

"Well, just get somebody else."

"Naw. This is the guy we want. This is Dutch's area. He knows him well, and I put my trust in Dutch. This isn't his first rodeo. He's a capable guy."

"Yeah, all right, all right. But you know, this fuckin' kid, he's gotta go!"

The mob gathering was at the Mirage. When we walked into the casino, Charlie spotted them gathered in the Race and Sports Book area. As soon as we appeared, they started sauntering over and greeting Charlie. There were eight or nine Lucchese family associates and some Genovese guys, one of whom was a fluffy-haired, chain-smoking New Yorker named Augie Lapari. I knew from Charlie's past comments that Lapari also had strong ties to the Gambinos.

For some reason, the guy latched on to me. "Giovanni Gatto? Gatto . . . Man, you look so familiar!" He eyed me closely through a pair of ill-fitting glasses that made him look like a cartoon. "Were we in the can together?" I shook my head, but he wouldn't let up. He studied me closely. "Yeah, we were locked up together, weren't we? You look real familiar!" He was half-drunk and loud, spouting off in front of every-body, and he was starting to arouse their interest in me.

This was the last thing I needed. "I don't think so." I feigned a puzzled look. "You ever do time in Virginia?"

"Naw. Lewisburg."

"I wasn't in Lewisburg, so . . . I don't know."

"But, man, you look so familiar! Giovanni Gatto, huh? All right, nice to meet you, Giovanni. So you know Charlie, huh? Charlie's friend?"

"Yeah."

Lapari kept it up, bombarding me with questions about my background, who my people were, where was my neighborhood. He was just an annoying tick in my ear, so I tried to stick close to my capo as he greeted the other guys. Charlie was definitely in his element, dressed to the nines and strutting around. He almost looked like Robert De Niro in *Casino*—the loud blazer, the slacks, the pocket square, the dark-rimmed eyeglasses—the picture of a 1960s Vegas gangster. I was cloaked in my typical button-down look: knife-edge slacks, designer shoes. I looked like a more modern-day gangster than the men I was meeting. They'd come to have a good time in Vegas, and their garb was more street-relaxed.

I asked Charlie what he would like to drink, and, to ingratiate myself, I offered everyone a round on me. Charlie noticed that gesture of respect and appreciated me spending my own money.

After a while, the group moved across the street to a cigar bar in Caesars. The plan was to sit in the little area outside, smoke cigars, and shoot the breeze. In the process, more guys showed up. One of them was "Johnnie Blue," a Genovese figure who was supposedly a multimillionaire. He was a polished guy, looking very much the part. He bought everyone a cigar, came over to see Charlie, shook my hand and said, "Nice to meet you," and then wandered off.

We were all sitting around smoking cigars—except Charlie, who was content with just a drink—when "Little Joe" Perna showed up. Perna was tall and lanky, but he looked more like a used car salesman than a mob boss. Despite the unprepossessing appearance, I knew him to be a Lucchese heavy. His arrival generated quite a scene, with some of the mobsters around me jumping up and shouting, "Hey! Little Joe's here! Little Joe! Hey, hey, Little Joe!" The Lucchese guys were all over him, sucking up.

While he was basking in this pathetic ritual, he spotted Charlie, and his whole demeanor changed. He broke free from the ring of ass-kissers and hurried over to where we were sitting. "Hey, Charlie, thanks for coming to see me! Really great you're here!" He seemed almost in awe of him.

Back in the day, Charlie had been very tight with Little Joe's father, Ralph, the head of the Luccheses' New Jersey faction. Joe sat down next to Charlie, and they started talking about the old days. They were speaking very quietly, and I was trying to listen in, but Augie Lapari, still a supreme nuisance, came over and interrupted my eavesdropping.

"So, Giovanni, where ya staying when you're here?"

"I'm at the ARIA."

"Oh yeah? That's a nice hotel. I like that hotel. So, where do you live?"

"I told you already, Augie. I live in New York."

"Oh, yeah, yeah, you did."

He was drinking and drinking and running his mouth. "You know, we ought to do some shit together. You know, while I'm out here, I got these hookers staying with me. Hired them to come stay with me. You should come out and party with us."

"I got my own thing out here, Aug, but thanks."

"Another thing . . . I came across these people the other day, these grifters in the casino."

"Grifters? What the fuck is a grifter?"

"You know, like the shanty Irish—like gypsies. They were trying to scam me. I'm thinking of maybe robbing these fucking people. You know, if you wanna rob them."

"I just met you! This is the dumbest . . ." It was obvious he was just being drunk and stupid, so I decided to break his balls. "Tell you what. If you get a chance, lure them back to New York and we can rob them there. Bring 'em onto our turf. If they're gypsies and they're moving around, tell 'em to call you when they get to New York, and we'll take care of them in our own backyard. How about that, Augie?"

"Yeah, yeah. That's a good idea. Maybe I'll do that, Giovanni." He dropped the subject and, soon after, wandered off to another table.

Charlie was still talking to Joe Perna, so I just sat there quietly. Some of the other guys strolled over and exchanged a few words with me, without really saying much. But I could feel them watching. They had seen my interaction with Augie, and now I was just sitting there silently, next to Charlie, smoking my cigar.

Charlie finished his drink.

"Charl, want another drink?"

"Naw, naw. I'm good."

"All right. Just wanted to make sure." I was just being his guy—and just making sure Little Joe understood that.

After a while, there was talk about everyone getting together later for a steak dinner, but by now I was thinking, *No fucking way*. There would be twelve to fifteen mob guys from three different crime families sitting around that table. For me, that would be way too much exposure. I made sure Charlie understood that I wouldn't be joining them. I just told him I was tired and needed to get some rest. By this stage of our relationship, I didn't need to dream up some elaborate excuse for not attending. Plus, if I insisted on being in on every meeting, that could generate suspicion.

Everybody said their good-byes, agreeing to meet later at Andiamo, an Italian steakhouse in the D Hotel, downtown on Fremont Street. But before Charlie had me drive him home, he wanted to have a private talk with Augie Lapari in his room at the Mirage. I was pretty tired of Lapari by now, so I wasn't too pleased with the idea. But I soon changed my mind.

Charlie and Augie hadn't seen each other in years, so the conversation started out with the two of them reminiscing. We were sitting in the hotel room, with me flopped in a lounge chair and them sitting at the table. They talked about a lot of topics—how things had changed, how the families interacted, who was running what, and who was in charge of this or that criminal enterprise. I was recording some really good intel for the LCN investigators.

Inevitably, Charlie started bragging to Augie about what he and I were doing. "I got this legitimate business going here. I'm looking to buy the Olympic Garden lounge. It's a casino and a strip club. If I can get that off the ground, it's gonna be great. And I'm trying to get a trucking thing going . . . our own trucking company. And Giovanni's got his swag thing, so . . ."

Augie turned to me. "Johnny, you got any Viagra in stock? Can you get me some? I can't keep up with these hookers!"

We all laughed, and I said, "No, Aug. But I'll see if I can find you some. I got some guys might be able to get it. I'll ask."

"Oh, you do? So what you do is, you give me a call when you get back to New York. I'm in Jersey. I got a little social club, and, you know, it's our family's thing, and you're always welcome there. Got a card game three nights a week. You should stop by."

"Yeah, maybe I will, Aug. Sounds good."

"Definitely call me, and bring me some samples. I'd love to do some business with you."

"Yeah, OK."

He gave me the address. "It's safe there. Nobody will bother you—really, really safe. Been there for years. The cops don't bother us. They know us."

When we left, I promised Augie I'd call him when I got home. As I drove Charlie back to his house, he was bubbling with enthusiasm. "Augie can take you to a lot of places!" Because I supposedly lived so close to Mulberry Street, Augie could introduce me to a guy named "Baby John," and another guy named Anthony from Brooklyn who had taken over all of Sammy the Bull's construction businesses. Everything that Sammy used to run, now this guy Anthony was running.*

Charlie effused, "This is going to be great! You're going to Mulberry Street. You're gonna meet my people, understand? They're my guys."

The conversation in Augie's hotel room had revealed valuable details of the interfamily structure—of how the Gambinos oversaw the DeCavs—and now I was being given an opportunity to move back and forth and marry them up on tape. But that level of activity would be a whole other animal, and it was something I decidedly would not do. All my years of experience in covert operations warned me that I wouldn't be able to control it. Charlie believed I lived close to the Mulberry Street action, but there was no way I was going to get mixed up with those

---

* Salvatore "Sammy the Bull" Gravano had been John Gotti's underboss—the mobster who, in 1991, famously cut a deal with federal prosecutors to testify against Gotti in return for a reduced sentence for his own crimes.

guys and with this lunatic Augie. Even if the case agents had asked me to do it (they didn't), I would have refused. I knew that level of involvement would prove to be unmanageable, and that's when things get extremely dangerous. I also knew, from talking to knowledgeable people, that there are buildings in that part of New York City—whole blocks of buildings—where the basements are interconnected. If, for any reason, some faction of mob guys decide they don't trust you, they lure you into one building, and your body comes out of some random basement at the other end of the street. During that drive back to Charlie's place in Henderson, I made a mental pledge to myself: *You will not go to Mulberry Street.*

The next day, Charlie and I took another ride into Las Vegas. On the way, I probed him a bit. "Those guys . . . you went to dinner with them last night?"

"Yeah. Didn't stay long. Just had dinner and went home."

I wanted to get from him how these mobsters saw me. "They were nice guys," I ventured, "but I'm not sure what they thought of me. They were giving me strange looks. I don't know if it was because they didn't trust me or what. And then Augie was asking me some weird fucking questions. So, I don't know, Charlie. You think I did all right? It was the first time I really represented you, I mean, being with you. I didn't want to seem like I was breathing down your neck."

"Naw! They all talked about you at dinner. They were asking about you."

"Asking about me?"

"Yeah. You scared the shit out of 'em!"

"I scared the shit out of *those* guys?"

"Giovanni! They fell in love with you. They were asking where you were. All of these guys did. Little Joe Perna was asking. Joe's the boss, you know that, right?"

"Yeah, but what was he saying?"

"He was asking about you because he was impressed. All his guys were sitting there shooting their mouths off. You weren't saying anything. You scared the shit out of them. Little Joe thought you were going to jump out of your seat if any of them made a wrong move at me. Figured you were going to kill 'em."

I laughed. "That's good."

"You kidding me? That's the way . . . you're *me*, my boy! You're me now! I love it! It's fucking great! A great thing."

That short conversation provided me with some meaningful affirmation. I was handling things right, staying in my lane, and—most important—impressing my boss.

31

NUT JOB AUGIE

AFTER I GOT BACK TO THE EAST COAST, Charlie kept badgering me to meet up with Augie. He said the guy had been calling him, saying, "Yeah, yeah, I can move some of that swag Giovanni has. He should come by my place and bring samples."

With some reluctance, I called Augie. He told me his daughter and son-in-law could move some of the stuff. He went on to explain that his son-in-law was a major cocaine supplier, in case I needed any. I pushed back on that, telling him I was good in that area and didn't need any new connections, but I agreed to come by his social club and drop off some samples.

I loaded up a couple of boxes and drove to the club. Augie was waiting for me outside. It was a typical Italian social club, situated right in the middle of a block. The windows were blacked out so that it was impossible for passersby to see in—tinted so dark, in fact, that from the inside I could hardly see out.

Augie unlocked the door and we went inside, both carrying the boxes I had brought. The interior was almost like a 1950s café— an old-style diner, with a counter and stools, card tables in the back, and a little kitchenette with a sink and fridge. A couple of guys were sitting there, reading newspapers. They looked like union guys—maybe construction workers—but one of them, with grayish hair, looked like an aging Irish thug. No one said hello. No one said anything to me at all, and Augie didn't bother to introduce me.

We sat down, and immediately he started in on me. "So, Giovanni, how do you know Charlie? How did you get to be with Charlie?"

"I met him through a couple of friends of mine. He knows some people, and . . . Why are you asking me that?"

"I'm just asking, like . . . I'm just asking, because I never heard of you."

"OK. I've been with him for a little bit . . . bouncing around. Through his nephew, I kind of met him, and that's how it went. So anyway, this is what we got . . ." I started opening boxes, showing him the North Face jackets, golf shirts, and women's tops that I had brought with me.

But he wasn't letting up. "So, where do you live?"

"I told you. New York."

"Yeah, no, like whereabouts? Charlie said you were in my neighborhood. Our guys, we're over on Mulberry Street, and you live close by, right? Where do you live? I don't know what street you live on."

"I didn't say what street I live on. But I live in the West Village."

"Oh, OK. Right. Yeah. It's a nice area, yeah, nice, nice. And, you did time, right?"

He hadn't even asked me if I wanted to get a drink, and here he was grilling me again. I showed him I was a little frustrated with his endless questions. "What the fuck, Aug? Really?"

I was uncomfortable with the two guys sitting down at the end of the bar. Augie was questioning who I was, and here was this one big guy who hadn't said boo to me, except to nod his head and go back to reading his paper. Why was he there? Why was the other guy there? When we came in, the outside door was locked. The place was closed.

I figured the best course was to check the rest of the club and make sure no one was hiding out in the back. I had dirt all over my hands from moving the boxes, so I said, "Augie, I've gotta wash my hands. I'm all dirty. You got a bathroom?"

"Yeah. In the back."

I knew I had to do it, but I was tormented by a nagging doubt. *Do you really want to risk walking out to the back?*

With my fears rushing at me like a swarm of bats, I stood up and headed toward the rear of the club. I couldn't help thinking about the conversation I'd had with Gooms about the "pop" of the gun when people got whacked.

Thank God, the back area was deserted. I washed up and returned to the front. Augie was still sitting where I left him, and the other two guys were gone.

"Hey, Giovanni, you want something to drink? A glass of wine."

It was eleven o'clock in the morning. "A little early for wine, no?"

"It's homemade wine."

"I'm not going to turn down homemade wine. Yeah, I'll have a glass with you. A small one."

"All right. You want a cannoli? I got cannolis left over from last night. We had the party. Had the girls here serving food."

"Yeah, if you got it. I'll have one, sure."

So, as we sat sitting there, sipping wine and eating cannoli, he returned to the old theme. "So, uh, where did you do your time? You were locked up, you say."

"Aug, come on! I told you when we were in Vegas! Fucking questions . . . you pepper me with questions! What's the matter with you? If you don't want to do business with me, don't do fucking business with me."

"Naw, naw! I'm just asking, just asking."

After that exchange, he left it alone. When I was leaving, he said, "I'll give the samples to my daughter. See if she can move them. We can do some business together."

Later that day, as I'd expected, Charlie called. "Hey, did you meet Goombah Augie today?"

"Yeah. I did." Signaling by my tone that I was aggravated, I added, "Yeah. I met the guy."

"How'd it go?"

"All right."

"What do you mean? What's the matter? Don't sound like it went all right."

"No, went all right. I gave him stuff, and that was that."

"Well, what's the matter?"

"Nothing. I just didn't fucking like the way he's questioning me. Asking me questions."

"What do you mean?"

"Asking lots of questions, saying things like he's doing his due diligence. Like, you know . . ."

"What are you talking about?"

"Kept asking how I met you, how long I'm around you, where I'm from, who I got arrested with, where I was locked up—shit like that."

"What the fuck is he asking that for?"

"I don't know. He's *your* friend, Charl! I don't know why he's asking. And, you know what, not for nothing you're my skipper. I only kept my mouth shut because he's your lifelong friend. Personally, if you ask me, the guy's an asshole."

"That motherfucker. I don't know. . . . What's he doing due diligence about?"

"I don't know. He said him and his friends wanted to do due diligence . . . something like that."

"Hmm. All right. Well, carry on, my boy. I'll talk to you later."

A few days later, I learned that Augie had been getting drunk and telling people that he did time with my father. So now he was just making up crazy shit—saying he was locked up with some gangster named Gatto who'd been around for a long time. According to Augie, my father was somebody named Joey "Streaky" Gatto, "a murderer, a stone-cold killer," and they'd done time together. He was making up this garbage and putting it on the street.

I heard about this from Danny Bertelli, who came to me and said, "What the fuck, I didn't know! Your father's Joey Gatto?"

"No. Where did you get that? Who's Joey Gatto?"

When I told Charlie about it, all he said was "Ah, it's just Augie. He's a little scatterbrained."

So I let it go. It wasn't as if I could do anything about it.

But then Charlie called me again. "Now I'm fucking mad!"

"What's the matter?"

"That fucking Augie. Now he's saying he don't know about you. He's asking questions about you. Warning people. Well, if he doesn't trust you, maybe that means he doesn't trust me!"

"Yeah."

"Well, you know . . . so here's what I want you to do. You go see him. I don't care if he's on fuckin' Mulberry Street or Timbuk-fuckin'-tu. You go to his club, or go to his place, and you take him a message from Charlie."

"What do you want me to tell him?"

"Tell him Charlie says he knows you a long time. He would do anything for you, but . . . go fuck your mother."

"That's your message, Charl? You want me to go into the Gambinos' house, or Augie's house, and tell Augie that in front of people? 'Go fuck your mother?'"

"Yeah. Tell him . . . you know what? If he thinks you're no good, and if he thinks I'm no good, then that makes me think that kid Joe that he's with, the one we were with the other day, also thinks I'm no good!"

I knew exactly who he was talking about: Little Joe Perna. But there were too many Joes in this case, so for evidence purposes I wanted him to say the full name to me. So I asked, "Who?"

"The kid! The kid we met. The kid Joe."

"Which Joe, Charl? Which Joe? Your Joe? Uncle Joey? Goombah Joey?"

"No. The kid we were dealing with. Joe."

"I don't know . . ."

"Jesus Christ, this fuckin' kid! Joe Perna! The kid we were with, Giovanni! Out here in Vegas."

"Oh, yeah! Yeah!" *That was a nice, tidy clarification for my recording.*

"Well, if Augie thinks I'm no good, you know what? Tell him to go fuck his mother."

"Charl, I'll deliver any message you want. I'll do whatever you tell me to. You want me to walk through fire, I'll walk through fire, but you want to rethink that message? Like, he's your lifelong friend. You know, it's Goombah Augie, and he's a fucking squirrel. I don't know him that long, but I can see that he's a little bit squirrelly, you know. He's stuck on stupid. He's a nut job. He might go over the edge."

"Yeah, yeah. Maybe you're right. You tell him, when he had fucking problems, who brought him to JoJo Ferrara? I did. I looked after him. He'd be dead in the water without me. So, if anything, he oughta be kissing my ass."

That message wasn't much better, but I would have to deliver it anyway.

Over the following days, Charlie kept asking, "You see Augie? You see the guy?"

I tried to blow it off. "No, not yet, Charl. I'm trying to get with him, but . . ."

Eventually, I was stuck making another trip to Augie's club to deliver some cigarette samples. Charlie himself had set up the meeting, and he pointedly reminded me of the message he wanted delivered.

I walked into the club, and once again some of Augie's associates were there, idling away their morning. I knew if I delivered Charlie's message right then and there, in front of that audience, things might not fare well for me. So I asked Augie to step outside to my Escalade to get the samples. Once we were out in the alley, where I had parked, I got ready to deliver Charlie's message.

"Augie, one second. I need to talk to you about something. You know, I'm with Charlie. He is a serious guy, but he's not all there in his head sometimes."

Augie had no idea where I was going with this, but I saw that I had his attention.

"You were asking me a lot of questions about my background. You said you were doing your due diligence on me, and now you've been telling people you knew my father. Well, I talked to Charlie about it and he's not happy."

With these words, Augie's expression suddenly transformed. He wore a look of sheer terror. He hastily interrupted me. "Hold on now, Giovanni! Please give me a second! Let me say something here!"

As I watched, he seemed to go into some kind of meltdown, breathing rapidly, as if he was having a panic attack. "Please Giovanni, I don't want any problems! I may drink a little too much sometimes and have a big mouth and say stupid shit."

He grabbed at his chest. I already knew he had heart problems, and I thought he might be having a coronary right there in front of me.

"Augie, take it easy. You're gonna have a friggin' heart attack."

"Giovanni, please, I meant no disrespect to you or Charlie! I don't want this! Let's talk here, OK?"

Then it hit me. Augie thought Charlie had given me the green light to whack him out for insulting me.

"Aug, do you think I'm here to hurt you?"

"*Pleeease*, Giovanni! Let's talk."

"Augie, listen. I would never hurt you, and Charlie would never hurt you. He loves you like a brother. He told me that himself. But when you say you wanted to do your due diligence, that pissed him off. He said he was there for you with JoJo, and he always looked out for you."

"He did, Giovanni!"

"He was super pissed at you. He wanted me to come here today and set it all straight. You know him, Aug. He always overreacts. He wanted me to come here and tell you to go your own way and that you should go fuck your mother. But I know he doesn't mean that. It's just his temper that gets the better of him."

"So are we good, Giovanni?"

"Yeah, we're good." I gave him a hard look. "If you can control yourself and stop the nonsense."

"Jesus Christ, I promise you got no problems with me, Giovanni!"

When I realized that Goombah Augie had truly believed that I was there to whack him out on Charlie's orders, I got a sense of what it felt like to be a true gangster, what it felt like to be feared. I couldn't comprehend how these people could live such a life, in constant dread, constantly worried about a betrayed friendship and plagued by the knowledge that someone they have known for decades could murder them in a moment of anger or irritation.

Even though I had clearly come out on top in that brief interaction, I was as determined as ever to keep my distance from Augie Lapari. And, happily, the stars aligned. Shortly after that conversation in the alley, he was involved in a serious car accident and, when our operation finally closed down, he was still recovering from his injuries.

I never had to deal with Nut Job Augie again.

32

WHACK THE DOG, ACT III

BY THIS STAGE OF THE OPERATION, I was flying out to Vegas with increasing frequency. And predictably, at some point during each visit, Charlie would work himself into a rage over Luigi Oliveri and the constant delays in killing him. On one of these occasions, when we were at his house in Henderson, I tried to appease him by saying that Dutch and Coop had been scoping out Luigi's neighborhood.

"They say he's got a card game." I knew about the card games at Luigi's social club, so when I said that, it sounded like the boys were doing their homework. "They checked the card game the other night, but he wasn't there. Then, the next night, they think they had him outside, walking down the street."

"Yeah, he does that! He doesn't drive. He walks home. Make sure you tell them that. He'll be walking with his guys. They might have to shoot a couple of people."

"All right."

"Unless they just go into his fucking club. If they can get one of them things—a grenade."

"What? A grenade?"

"Yeah. If you got any military connections. I can't get them, but you could get one of them things."

"Well, one of those things the cops use. A flash bang or something?"

"Yeah, something like that."

"I can't get hold of a real grenade. I don't want to blow a whole fucking building up."

"Yeah, you don't want to blow everybody up. Well, whatever they need to do." He looked at me. "Do they even know for sure who he is?"

By asking that, Charlie gave me the perfect opening. If I could get him to give me a photo of Luigi, that would help our case against him, so I said, "They're saying everybody down in that neighborhood looks like the Dog. We're Italian, Charl. We all look the same to those biker guys, right?"

"Yeah. What they need is a picture. You need to give them a picture."

"Maybe I can get a picture from Whitey."

"Nah, don't ask fucking Whitey nothing. Don't involve him with this."

"Well, he was trying to get me the wheels, but I told him don't worry about it."

"And the guns . . . ?"

"Dutch is going to take care of the weapons. He's got it all covered. But, like you say, it's just the problem of making sure they got the right guy."

We were having this discussion in the living room, with the TV on, and Patty was in bustling around in the kitchen. Charlie yelled to her. "Patty! *Patty!*"

"What?"

"The Dog. The Pet. You got pictures of the Dog?"

"Luigi?"

"Yeah."

"No. Why would I have pictures of Luigi?"

"Can you get one? Why don't you go on the computer with your friends, the girls? Don't you got that Facebook shit?"

"Oh, yeah, yeah."

She went to the computer. He got off the couch and stood over her, "Yeah, yeah. There you go. Print that one and that one."

She printed off two pages on 8½-by-11 sheets. Charlie got a pair of scissors and trimmed them down to a smaller size. He handed the two photos to me. "Here you go. Give these to your guys."

Every word was recorded.

On another front, my frequent visits to Vegas were creating complications, because I was beginning to attract law enforcement surveillance. I don't think I was personally doing anything to bring attention to myself, but the inescapable fact was that Charlie's federal probation had been transferred to Las Vegas. In such cases, local law enforcement is notified that a federal parolee is residing in its jurisdiction. So, we had the Las Vegas Metro Police, the Nevada State Police, and other federal divisions that were unaware of our FBI operation—all of them looking to monitor Charlie and make sure nobody's in a casino who shouldn't be.

All of which meant I had to be careful when Charlie was around. I often said to him, "We've got to watch where we go. You're not really supposed to be around me, Charl. You're on parole, and I'm a convicted felon." He already believed that I'd done time, but it made sense to check that box once in a while. I was saying, "I'm watching your back, boss. I'm doing what Patty asked me to do." It also gave me some justification for saying, "Hey, maybe we should just take a step back this time."

One day, while I was staying at the ARIA Hotel, Charlie called me for a pickup. I exited the lobby and asked the valet to get my car. The casino was packed, and a lot of people were standing around waiting for their vehicles. It wasn't my habit to check myself for a tail, but three guys hanging around near me were so blatantly obvious, I couldn't help but notice them. They were wearing a specific selection of civilian attire that gave them away as plainclothes cops: 5.11 Icon cargo pants, baseball caps, cheap golf shirts, and backpacks. The one standing nearest to me was obviously armed—I could see the bulge on his hip under his shirt.

I was standing there, waiting for my car, and this one guy was not going away. Another member of the team was sitting on a bench, and a third guy was standing nearby. They didn't seem to be waiting for anyone or for a car, and they had no idea how to blend in. I mean, even if you're a cop with a gun on your hip, at least stand there with a ticket in your hand. Not one of them was holding a valet ticket. They were already there when I came out of the hotel, and yet their car is still not here? All the other people ahead of me were getting their cars.

I decided to screw with them.

I walked away about twenty yards and then abruptly reversed course and strode back into the hotel. Wouldn't you know it, the one who had been closest to me followed me right through the glass doors and into the lobby. I walked around a little bit, leading him astray, and then slipped back outside. Now another one of these idiots came and stood close to me. A few seconds later, the one I had ditched in the lobby came back outside. The real joke was that they were all on their cell phones. Obviously, they were talking to each other.

Now that I was certain that all three were cops, I knew I had to get them off me. I pulled out my phone and put it to my ear as if I were answering a call. I started walking and talking, purposely passing near one guy who was leaning against a concrete pillar. "Yeah, yeah," I said. "Just waiting for my car now. Getting my car." I looked at the guy, and as soon as I made eye contact with him, he scurried away. He was an obvious novice, afraid to get burned, with no clue that he'd been burned from the start.

Still playing make-believe on my phone, I walked past another one. "Sorry. Yeah, yeah. Fifteen minutes. I don't know. The car's coming. Should be here in a couple of minutes. Yeah, same place, by that Starbucks, the one by that Chinese place. That's right . . . down off Fremont. Give me fifteen minutes." A couple of days earlier, I'd been to the location I was describing. It was in the opposite direction from my intended route of travel.

Just then, with perfect timing, my car arrived. I jumped behind the wheel and drove out of the valet area fast, practically skidding around the corner.

Although I'd cleaned myself off pretty easily, it was clear that my presence had been noticed. Whether I'd been seen and noticed with Charlie, or with Dutch and Coop, or whatever it was, I had attracted

unwanted attention. On one level, it didn't matter. I wasn't doing anything illegal. I wasn't transporting drugs. I wasn't doing anything that
could get me arrested. Still, because of this local law enforcement interest, my whole way of living out in Vegas would have to change. I would
have to be extra watchful. We couldn't afford to have some Metro or
state cops following me, and I couldn't count on all of them being rank
amateurs like the three I'd just shaken.

During that same trip, I had a revealing interaction with Patty. The three
of us were planning to head out for dinner. Patty and I were alone downstairs while Charlie was up in the bedroom getting changed. She looked
me in the eye and said something odd. "Giovanni, you need to stay away
from Jimmy Dirt. I know Charlie tells you to go see Jimmy Dirt, but
whatever you do, Giovanni, stay away from him. Don't go near him."

"Jimmy Dirt" was the street name of a DeCav soldier named Jimmy
Castaldo.

"Why?"

"Because he's going to get arrested."

"He is? For what?"

"The feds are on him. He's getting arrested any day now. Hold on
. . . I'll show you something." She went to her computer and returned
with a large manila envelope. "See. Look at this."

She pulled out a document and handed it to me. It was a faxed
copy of a US District Court, District of New Jersey, criminal complaint
against James Castaldo. It hadn't been stamped yet, and it hadn't been
signed by a judge, but Patricia Malone, the live-in girlfriend of mob
capo Charlie Stango, had a copy of it.

We'd suspected for some time that there was a law enforcement leak,
and here in my hand was the evidence. My recording devices were running, so I kept the talk going in order to get some of the details on tape.

"So, what the fuck is this?" I asked, playing dumb.

"It's a federal complaint. See . . . 'United States of America' . . . 'Criminal Complaint.'"

I held the document in front of me and got her to answer more dim-witted questions: "OK, I don't get this. . . . What's this number up here? So that's what they call a docket number? Oh shit. This is like 'United States of America versus . . .' Yeah, look at that. Jimmy Castaldo, huh? No kidding. So this is, like, a criminal complaint? The real thing?"

"Yeah."

"Who's this here?"

"Oh, that's the magistrate judge that's gonna sign it . . . stamp it. As soon as they stamp it, it's going to be done. So how do you like that, huh? I got it. See, I look out for all of you guys."

"No kidding!"

"That's what I told you. I'm watching out for you guys. I'm always looking out."

"Great, but how did you get that?"

"My girlfriend sent it to me."

She slid it back in the envelope, walked it back over to her computer, and laid it on top of the printer. Later, when I got ready to leave Vegas, I told the cover agents, "She has a criminal complaint in that house that hasn't been stamped yet, so when you guys hit the house and pick up Charlie, you need to grab it." I told them exactly where it was and who it related to, and I also told the case agents back in New Jersey.

Weeks later, at the end of the operation, I found out that they had never bothered looking for it. They sent agents from the Las Vegas FBI office to Henderson to arrest Charlie Stango, accompanied by one agent from New Jersey, but none of them thought to grab it—sloppy work. That document could have revealed who the actual leak was inside the federal system. It also could have been used by the case agents as a bargaining chip when they were interviewing Charlie. If he believed Patty was going to be arrested and thought he could save her by full cooperation, he might have spilled a lot more than he did. But I guess that just wasn't important enough for some.

33

HOTSY-TOTSY SHRIMP

THE OPERATION WAS COMING TO AN END. It was only a matter of weeks, maybe even days. I knew it, but of course Charlie Stango and Patricia Malone did not.

By now, on the personal level, things were going well between me and Charlie and Patty. I guess I should say *too well*. We had become almost a family—truly, truly, treating each other like family. Patty loved me. She was texting me constantly: "When are you coming back out? It's cold out there. It's eighty degrees here and you got snow. Come here, Giovanni! Live here!"

I'd be in Vegas, getting ready to fly back to the East Coast, and Patty would be tugging at my sleeve. "Giovanni, you sure you want to fly out tonight? You should stay here! It's snowing back east. It's really bad! They're three feet under snow."

"Yeah, Patty, I know. But I gotta get back. I've got a lot of things to do for Charl."

"Be sure you call as soon as you land! You don't have to, but if you would, please? Just let us know you got home OK."

Charlie would always walk me out through the garage, and I'd get in my rental car, and he'd say, "Hey, hey! Did you get your water?"

"No. I'm going right back to the hotel."

"Naw, naw. It's hot here, Giovanni. Take a water. Matter of fact, take two waters." He'd run in and grab them out of the fridge. "Ya gotta stay hydrated out here. Remember what I told ya, right? Be careful driving, right?"

"All right, Charl."

There is no way around it and no way I can pretend otherwise: I was welcomed into their home and their lives, and each time I left Nevada, I had increasing feelings of guilt that I struggled to suppress. I knew I had to be careful with what I said, because everything was being recorded. But this murderous gangster, Charlie Stango, kept demonstrating how much he loved me, and in those last few months of the case, he was actually saying it:

"Aw right, Charl. Thanks for everything, Charl."

"Be careful driving once you get there."

"I will."

"All right. I love you, kid."

"I love you too, Charl."

What else could I say? It was true. Moments like that made me feel like a piece of shit. These people kept telling me how much they cared about me, and they were genuinely worrying about me.

One night, I took Charlie and Patty out to a nice restaurant in the Bellagio. I had arranged for a special table where we could watch the fountains. I had tried for the best seat in the house, overlooking the fountains, but had to settle for second best because a couple who were celebrating their fiftieth wedding anniversary had beat me to it.*

On this particular evening, Charlie was in fine spirits, and as soon as we sat down, he "pulled a Giovanni," as he called it. Months earlier, shortly after we had first met, he had listened with amusement as I ordered a particular drink that I liked. He'd smirked at my fussiness when placing the order, but after eventually trying the drink himself, he found that he liked it.

Once we were seated, a young waiter came over and asked the usual question: "Can I get you folks started with some drinks?"

---

* Not that Charlie would necessarily appreciate the view. Long experience with him had taught me that he had no idea how to act properly in a fine restaurant. More than once he had embarrassed me with his conduct—telling waiters their food was garbage and sending managers scurrying away, trailed by an onslaught of foul language.

Charlie said, "You know what? I'm gonna have . . . Do you have Hendricks?"

"Yes sir."

"Get me a Hendricks and tonic—with a lime. And give me a seltzer backer."

The waiter appeared genuinely impressed. "You want to back it with a seltzer, sir?"

"Yes, I want a seltzer backer."

The kid looked at him and said, "I'm impressed by the way you order your drink, sir. You're a man who knows what he wants."

Charlie looked startled. "Huh? Well, thank you."

After the waiter left, Charlie gave a little guffaw. "Hah, see that? I did a Giovanni! Like that, hey? Like that?"

We ordered our meals, and Patty and Charlie were doing their usual routine—sniping at each other, but in a good-natured way. But later in the meal, Charlie started getting calls on his cell phone, and from that point things went rapidly downhill.

With Charlie busy on his phone, Patty started asking me questions. "Giovanni, are you really going to move out here when the club opens? When we get this club off the ground?"

"Yeah, I'm moving out here. That's what he wants, so that's what I'm going to do."

"You really would leave New York? What about Lena?"

"Well, Lena's either going to come or she's going to stay. I don't know what she's going to do, and I'm not going to worry about it. Lena always does what Lena wants. I'm coming here, and I'm going to run the Olympic Garden with Charlie."

"Well, we've got to find you a place to live . . . a townhouse or something."

"We'll start looking. If you want to walk around tomorrow, we'll look."

Then, as we were talking, she asked, "What about your family?"

"What do you mean?"

"Where's all your family? Is your family back in New York, or Florida, or Atlantic City? Where do they live?"

222 GIOVANNI'S RING

"No, Patty, don't worry about that."

"Well, don't you have family? Brothers and sisters?"

"No. No brothers or sisters. I'm an only child." Charlie was still on the phone, not listening to us, so I added, "I don't have a family. He didn't tell you?"

"Tell me what?"

"That I don't have . . . Of course, I have a mom and dad."

"Oh, are they alive? Where do they live?"

"I don't know. My dad . . ." I took a deep breath. "I can't believe he never told you this."

Now I had piqued her interest. "Well, no."

"My dad? I never knew my father. Apparently he was in Vietnam, and all my mom ever told me was that when he came back from the war he was a junk box. He was hooked on dope, or . . . smoking dope, and then just became an addict. I don't know . . . heroin or something. He came back, and, you know, that's where my life came from. My dad ran with outlaw bikers and dragged my mom and me around like nomads."

"Ah, oh, OK."

"So, eventually he wasn't around because, I think . . . I don't know whether he just left, or my mom left him. I was raised by . . . pretty much by my mom. I never asked her for the story about why they split up, because I didn't care. All I knew was that he was a junkie, and he was no good. All I ever got from him was his name, so fuck him. I don't care."

"Where's your mom live?"

"Oh, Mom's not with me anymore."

"Oh, my God! I'm so sorry, Giovanni."

I could see her spiraling down, looking more and more depressed by my invented background, so I decided to draw on that and start to look emotional. Even vulnerable. "It's all right, Patty. Don't worry about it. It's all right." I shrugged my shoulders and slowly lowered my head. "It's all right. It's just . . . she's . . . I don't know."

"What happened? Did she get sick?"

"No. You know, it's just that . . . Mom was good to me. She tried her best, but I grew up in an environment that was . . . I think the word people use is *toxic*. My dad wasn't there, and my mom was always hooking up with some biker, or some random guy, whether it was a trucker, or a . . . She didn't know any better. She tried her best, but she couldn't provide for me."

"Oh, that's so sad!"

I brightened a bit. "But, you know, fast forward to today. My mom screwed up a lot, but that's when my cousin Coop . . . I told you about Coop? Charlie met him that day we had breakfast at Raffles."

"Yeah, I remember!"

"Well, my cousin Coop, he's not really my cousin, I call him my cousin because he's the only family I had. Our moms were best friends, and when mine went off partying and was missing for days . . . I really don't know if she was doing dope, or meth, or whatever she was doing back then. While my mother was missing, I would stay with Coop and his mom. Then my mother would come home, and then everything would be good again."

"That's terrible, Giovanni."

"Well, she tried her best. But I think I found out years later that she suffered from, like, that bipolar type thing, whatever they call it. And that's why she was fucked up. She loved me to death, but she just couldn't . . ." I started thinking about something sad from my own life—my real life—and started welling up.

But I quickly realized I had gone too far.

"Oh, that's just terrible!" Patty exclaimed, and she started crying— not just a few tears running down her face, but crying and gasping.

"Patty, please stop! You're gonna get me going. I don't really like to talk about this stuff, and now you're gonna get me going." I picked up a napkin and put it to my face and wiped a tear, and I said, "Stop it. You're making me look weak, and I don't like it. So knock it off."

"But that's fucking horrible, Giovanni. I'm so sorry!"

"Don't worry, Patty. Listen, everything is good. I grew up. I'm here. I'm fine."

"Yeah, but you don't have any family. That's a horrible thing."

"What are you talking about?" I lowered my voice. "I got family. I got you, and I got Charlie."

"What?"

"Yeah, listen, I've got you guys. I don't need nothing else. Look where I am. Like, he's the dad," I whispered. "He's the father . . . he's the father I never had."

Patty started to cry again, and a second later, disaster struck.

Charlie was on a flip phone, and he suddenly snapped it shut, signaling his call was over. He took one look at Patty's face, and lit into her.

"What the fuck's wrong with you?" he snapped. "Mad because I'm on the phone again? Gonna break my balls?"

She turned on him. "*You motherfucker!*"

All around us, heads turned as they started yelling at each other, getting louder and louder. Here we had those poor people at the table next to us, trying to enjoy their fiftieth anniversary, and they had to listen to these two New Jersey animals throwing F-bombs at one another and ruining everything.

I jumped in, saying, "Just calm down. Everybody hold on. Calm down. Please!"

"You know what?" Patty bawled. "Now I just want to go the fuck home!"

Charlie barked back. "No! Let's eat. Let's finish dinner."

She looked him in the face and hissed, "I was talking to Giovanni, and he was telling me something sad, so fuck you!"

Charlie left it alone after that, and in an atmosphere of lingering tension, we somehow got through the meal.

The next morning, Charlie called me at my hotel and demanded that I come to the house.

"What's the matter? Everything all right?"

"How long are you gonna be before you get here? I need you here now!"

His tone seemed strained. Something was going on, and it sounded important.

"As soon as I get dressed, I'm coming."

"How long?"

"I don't know. How long does it take me to get dressed? I'll be there in . . . forty-five minutes."

"*Jesus Christ!* Hurry the fuck up!"

"Give me a half-hour! I'll be there in a half hour!"

So now I had to run. I didn't know what he wanted, but it sounded important. I had to run to a nearby hotel to get the recorders from the cover agents, run back to my hotel to get my car, and then head over to Henderson.

I knocked on the door and walked in. There was no Patty, just Charlie, standing in the kitchen. I said good morning and gave him the kiss.

"Sit down. You eat?"

"Naw, you just woke me up. Where's Patty?"

"She ain't here." He was really abrupt, almost short with me. Not comfortable at all.

"OK."

"Sit down! Sit down here." He pointed to the only chair that had a place setting.

I immediately decided I wasn't going to sit there, so I pulled up a chair on other side of the table.

"The fuck you doin'? I'm sitting there! Sit over there!"

I got up and moved.

Now I was concerned. He was talking to me in quick, short phrases, and his manner was stiff, really weird compared to his usual demeanor. Something felt horribly wrong, but I couldn't fathom what it was. The atmosphere just didn't feel right to me. It felt almost dangerous.

"I made breakfast," he said.

What? Charlie doesn't cook. Where's Patty?

"Sit down. I'll get your coffee." He brought the pot over and filled my cup. "I didn't make it like Patty, I don't know how to do what she does, but I made you coffee."

I tasted it. "It stinks," I said. But behind my grin, my mind was racing, thinking the worst. I didn't know where Patty was. I didn't know if something had gone bad, if something about me had leaked out.

Did he have another bad dream? Did the Administration cancel the hit on Luigi? Did they decide to get rid of anyone who had knowledge of what they'd been planning? I was on my own in Charlie's house with no eyes on me.

These alarm bells were ringing in my head when he said, "I made hotsy-totsy shrimp. You ever have hotsy-totsy shrimp?"

"No. What the fuck is that?"

"Oh? You never had it?"

"No. What is it?"

"You like spicy food?"

"Yeah, a little bit."

"Ah, my mother used to make it. You'll love it."

And just as I was thinking the worst, he took my plate, went to the stove, and scooped up a big helping of something. He returned it to the table, heaped with shrimp.

"You want bottled water?"

"Yeah, I'll get it," and I got out of my chair.

"Sit down! Sit down! I'll get it. I'll get the fucking water!" He opened the fridge, got a bottle of water, cracked the cap for me, and put the bottle in front of me. "Ah, you need milk—milk for your coffee, right?"

By now I was convinced he was getting ready to whack me out.

"Forget the milk, Charlie. Aren't you going to sit? Aren't you going to eat?"

"Naw, naw. I ate before. I'm done eating."

"So I'm eating by myself?"

"Yeah, yeah. Eat. You'll like it. Tell me if you like it."

As he sat down directly across from me, I was acutely aware that the sliding patio doors behind me were open to the yard. Again, I couldn't help thinking the worst: *This is where the guys hiding in the yard come in and dispose of me.*

So I took a bite of what I thought might be my last meal—and it was absolutely delicious. As I dug in, he folded his arms on the table, and just watched me.

"So, you like it? It's good, right?" He was staring right at me.

"Yeah, it's good. Really good, Charl. Delicious!"

"Yeah, I love that shit. My mother used to make that for me. Right there is my favorite meal in the world. Love it, love it!"

"Yeah, it's good. I'll have to get this recipe."

"I'll give you the recipe." A few seconds went by. Then he said, "Fucked up night we had, last night. Patty getting under my skin in the restaurant."

"Yeah, yeah."

"So that's it. You and me, we're going to have some good things going on." Before my eyes, he seemed to transform. He became Mr. Giddy, Mr. Happy Pants, telling me all these great things that were going to happen in my life, all these positive things: the investor with the cash would come through, the glacier we would own, the club we would to buy . . . everything was going to be a home run. And on and on and on.

Patty came home while I was still trying to figure out what was going on with this happy, babbling chatterbox version of gangster Charles Stango sitting across the table from me. Patty took one look at my plate and said, "You're eating the hotsy-totsy shrimp? Wow! That's Charlie's mom's dish!"

"Yeah. I love it."

Charlie beamed. "I don't cook for everybody, right, Patty?"

"I appreciate it, Charl," I said. "Thanks. It's a lot better than eating diner food somewhere that I was going for breakfast."

"All right. I just wanted you to know what you mean to me, so I cooked for you." He got up. "I'm gonna go get dressed."

Patty pulled up a chair. "Him making that for you . . . that's special. We came home last night, and he yelled at me, 'What the fuck were you crying about,' and I told him why I was upset. I told him what you said."

"You told him?"

"Yeah. I told him what you said. And, you know, that meant a lot, and he got a little choked up by it. So I think he just wanted to do something special for you. He thinks the world of you. You know that, Giovanni? He's got that idiot of a son, Anthony, and his other son, who doesn't talk to him much, so it's good that you guys have each other. He loves you."

Sometimes, despite yourself, despite knowing you're absolutely doing the right thing getting dangerous criminals off the street . . . sometimes doing this job can really make you feel like the scum of the earth.

34

ENDGAME

CHARLIE KEPT PRESSING ME ABOUT THE HIT ON LUIGI, and I finally ran out of excuses. In what would become our final conversation on the subject, I told him that my guys were ready.

We were at his house in Henderson. I said, "OK, Charl. That's it. When I get home, I'm calling them up. I'm going to meet them. I'm going to tell them it's on. We're going to do it."

"That's good. So, when do you think?"

"A matter of days. They're in the area, so they're ready to go. As soon as they find him and they fucking put him down, we're done. Done."

Charlie couldn't have been more excited. He was beep-bopping around and chuckling. "Ah, this is fucking great! Fucking great, Giovanni!" It was like he was killing Luigi himself. "But, you know, you be careful. You gotta tell these guys to be careful. You gotta watch what you do . . ." He didn't want me to get caught like he did.

"But once he's gone, how does that leave us? Think they're gonna look at me?"

"Nobody's even gonna think of you."

"You don't think he's down there in the neighborhood telling everybody he has a problem with me?"

"No. You're not his problem. The outfit is. And they're waiting to get him. You just go out there, get the guys, make sure they use the pictures. If he's in the coffee shop, you walk in, boom, boom, and you walk the fuck out. You know, it's the quickest way."

"Yeah, that's the way to do it."

"He's always got a couple of guys with him, ya understand. So if your guys come in with, you know, saying 'This is a stickup,' *boom, boom, boom,* and just walk out. Just walk the fuck right out, get in the car, and go. OK?"

"Yeah."

"Have a fucking car waiting! Ya gotta have somebody waiting on the street, you know. And you want a car you can just drop off. Cops can't trace it. You're gonna drop it off and then get in another car and go."

"Yeah, that's a good idea too."

"You do it at night. The Pet's always out at night, so if he's in the coffee shop at night, sometimes there won't be nobody there except two or three other guys. You walk in, and that's it. There's four guys. 'Don't nobody move!' They got his picture—*boom, boom, boom,* tough guy, *boom, boom, boom.* That's how I would do it."

"Good thought. And the two guys, Charlie. Dutch and the other guy. They'd never . . . if something should go wrong, they never would say nothing."

"Well, yeah. Gotta take care of them wherever the fuck they are."

When I left, he walked me out through the garage, saying, "Just let me know. When it's done, I gotta know right away. I gotta know so I can let everybody else know."

"How do you want to do that? You want me to call you?"

"Yeah. Just call me. Just let me know."

"You want me to use something like: 'My girl Lena's upset because she had to put her dog down last night?' You know: 'It got sick and we took it to the vet. Had to put the dog down.'" I thought that sounded like a good idea—the dog, the pet, put down. I mean, to me that sounded pretty ingenious.

"Nah! Whatever time of night it is, whenever it is, three o'clock in the morning, whenever. Just call me up and tell me . . . uh . . . tell me you washed your face."

"What? You want me to just say that?"

"Yeah. Just tell me, 'Hey, it's me. I washed my face.'"

I thought that was pretty weird, but I just said, "All right."

We said our good-byes in the garage. That was the hardest time for me. I just wanted to tell him who I was. I'd had visions about this moment the night before, and would again for many nights after. I still think about it, standing there with him in his garage. I wanted so badly to tell him. I wanted to say, *Charl, make a phone call. Turn yourself in now. Call the US attorney. Make a deal. Keep yourself out of jail. I am so sorry.* How sad is that?

But I couldn't help it. I kept telling myself this was Charlie. He wasn't planning to blow up a building. He wasn't like these other people we dealt with—al-Qaeda cells incinerating innocent people, or trigger-happy goons pulling off bank jobs. The guy he was plotting to kill was inside the thing that they both belonged to, and he knew the possible consequences. Yeah, Charlie was wrong for planning the murder, but Lui the Dog knew what he'd signed up for. He'd wanted his button, and he got it. He knew exactly what kind of an organization it was, and getting whacked was one of the occupational hazards that came with membership.

"Safe landing," Charlie said. "Call me when you get there. Let me know you got there OK."

"I'll call you as soon as I get home," I promised.

It was strange, because looking back, I know I was just trying to drag it out. Drag out the good-bye. I knew that was the last time I'd see Charlie face to face. I kissed him three times, and I hugged him, and I gave him a hard, long squeeze. It's almost like I was trying to tell him something. If he'd been paying attention to my body language, he would have seen it. He should have seen it, but by now his radar was turned off. I had lulled him to sleep.

He gave me a smack on the back of my neck. "All right, my boy! See ya later. Be careful driving."

"Love ya."

"I love you too. Just make sure you call when you get back."

When he said, "I love you too," I almost lost it.

I got in my car with tears welling in my eyes. As I backed out of the driveway, he was still standing there, adjusting his sweatpants, watching me. Watching "his boy."

I felt sick. I knew it was the end of Giovanni Gatto. And I knew it was the end of Charlie Stango.

It was hard to drive away, back to Las Vegas, and to drive along the Strip. It didn't feel victorious. It didn't feel soothing.

Yes, I felt complete as far as the case was concerned. Yes, I had done my job. But the human being inside this cop felt like shit.

My case agents wanted to go for a drink somewhere quiet—a drink to celebrate, they said. I wanted nothing to do with it and nothing to do with them. I just wanted to be alone. Short of me making a couple of calls when I got home and cleaning up a few loose ends, the operation was over.

Except it wasn't over. It would never be over.

35

ARREST

WHAT I BELIEVED had been my last trip to Vegas . . . wasn't.

The case agents asked me to fly back out for the arrest. "We might be able to use you there, in case he decides not to flip or doesn't believe you are who we say you are." They wanted to do a "Donnie Brasco" on him: drop my name, throw my picture down, walk me into the room, maybe sit me across the table from him, and see if I could convince him to cooperate.

It was a brutal prospect, but I did harbor a private hope that I could get in front of Charlie. Was I looking for atonement? Was I seeking to do penance?

Yes, I was.

I returned to Las Vegas as requested and booked myself at the Vdara Hotel, which is located behind the ARIA. But in the end, the agents never called for me. I spent three days in that city with nothing to do, nowhere to go, and nobody to meet—no Dutch, no Coop, no Charlie, no agents. Nobody. I didn't even have authority to rent a car. All I did was walk around, revisiting the places Charlie and I had frequented, eating in the same restaurants, thinking of him, thinking of Patty, of Whitey, of Danny Gooms and Marco Barone, thinking of Dutch and Coop—and thinking of Anna and our children. Wandering around Las Vegas with nothing to do but drink.

Charlie Stango was arrested at five o'clock in the morning on March 12, 2015. He was always an early riser—even two years after his release, he was still on prison time, so when the agents arrived he was already up and dressed. He went quietly. Within hours, the story was all over the news. In every bar I walked into—and, yes, there were many—the TV was on. News anchors were interviewing talking heads, so-called organized crime experts, self-important *chooches* grinning into the camera, spouting their opinions. None of them had any idea that the agent who was behind it all was watching them, listening to their self-important drivel, and drinking himself into oblivion.

In the interview room, the first few minutes didn't go exactly as the agents might have planned. Everything was filmed, and I've seen the tape. They told Charlie he'd been arrested for conspiracy to murder, for racketeering, and for a laundry list of other offences.

He responded by saying, "All right. Can I use the bathroom?"

He went to the bathroom, executed his regular morning dump, and didn't bother to flush. Soon, the stench was wafting into the room where the agents were setting up.

One of them said, "What the hell? Smells horrible in here!"

Charlie laughed. "Ah! See that? That's what I think of the federal government."

One of the junior agents was dispatched to flush the toilet.

Meanwhile, in New Jersey, everyone implicated over the years of our operation was waking up to teams of FBI agents armed with search warrants pounding on their doors. When the agents entered Whitey Stango's house, he whispered to his girlfriend, "Take my phone. Call Giovanni. Tell him to run." Whitey had no idea that his father was already in custody, sitting in a processing room in Las Vegas. He thought the targets were just him and me. The agents caught the girl as she was going for Whitey's phone. They stopped her, but they didn't arrest her.

It was several days before the New Jersey arrestees learned that Charlie Stango's right-hand man—Cugine Giovanni, "Coz," "Uncle G" to Whitey's kids—was an FBI undercover officer. Some of them, like Mario Galli, flatly refused to believe it. And it was several days before Luigi "the Dog" Oliveri learned that the man he had plotted to maim or kill in the basement of his social club had repaid the favor by saving his miserable life.

But Charlie Stango was told immediately. The agents wanted him to know who I was and what I was. After telling him, they left him alone in the interview room. The camera kept running, looking down on him, and I've watched this part of the tape over and over.

For long seconds, he sat there, very still. He put his head back and stared at the ceiling. Then he said, "Ah, Patty, Patty! Patty! Sorry, Patty!" He rubbed his eyes, and repeated, "Oh, Patty. I'm sorry, Patricia. I'm sorry." He leaned back further, rubbing his face, and said, "I'm sorry, Patty. Jesus Christ!" And then he raised his voice: "Fucking Giovanni! Giovanni! Wash your face, Giovanni! Wash your fucking face!"

I don't know for certain what he meant, but I can guess: *Go kill yourself!* or *I hope you fucking die!*

I stayed in Las Vegas for an extra day. My case agents were gone, Charlie was locked up, and Patty was stewing in their house. I spent the day sitting by the hotel pool. I just wanted to be alone.

And then I flew back to New Jersey. When I walked off the plane, I had nothing to do related to the job, no reason to go to the office, nothing like that.

I went home to my wife and my kids.

36

HOME ALONE

At the end of it all, I knew I would have to be relocated, meaning our entire family had to move. And this is where it all went off the rails, because there seemed to be no set procedure for a task force officer. At least there wasn't for me. At the end of the operation, when the team was getting ready to do the takedown, I wasn't even in consideration. I was sitting in on a meeting at the US Attorney's Office, right before the big day, and the attorney asked, "OK, any other things we need to clarify before we issue arrest warrants?"

"No."

"Well, do we have any informants, any sources that we need to relocate, or put under protection for now, or . . . ?"

"Naw. We're good." I was sitting in that room, in plain view down at the end of the table, and they were saying, "We're good."

My supervisor said, "Well . . . ah . . . there's Giovanni. What are we doing with him?"

"Oh? Oh, yeah, yeah, um, right. I guess we're going to think about that. Well, ah, hmm . . . OK, we'll look into that. We'll have to seriously do something with that."

And that was it. They were still "looking into that" after all the defendants had been arrested and were lining up for detention hearings. No planning was in place to ensure my safety or my family's safety. The defendants eventually did make bail, and some were released under house arrest, with a bracelet on. But me? I came out of my undercover role and ended up stuck in my house. I was told, "Get your family back in order; get your affairs in order; do what you gotta do. And maybe grow a beard to change your appearance, so you don't have to duck and dodge around." That was the best they could come up with.

Anna had warned me. She had warned me again and again. And she had been right.

I ended up sitting in our house, growing that beard. In the aftermath of the operation, I was as much under house arrest as the defendants—more so, in fact, because they were allowed out to go shopping. Of course, I wasn't officially confined to the house, but where was I going to go? Luigi and some of the others were out on bail and living in nearby communities. When Luigi listed the address where he was going to reside during his release, it turned out to be in very close proximity to our home.

And then there was Patty. After Charlie was taken away, she came back to New Jersey. Nobody bothered to tell me she was moving. I only learned about it by accident when the case agent called me.

"Anything new?" I asked.

"Naw. Nothing new. Oh, yeah . . . there is one thing. I forgot to tell you. Patricia is living by you. I think she's in the general area. I'll get the address and call you."

He texted me the address. I googled it—too close for comfort.

I called him back. "Are you kidding me? Don't you think that was important enough to tell me right away? You know, she's shopping in the same malls, shopping everywhere my family goes! What if I'd taken a chance and gone shopping with my wife and kids and she'd spotted me?"

I spent hours on the living room couch, waiting for phones to ring. The only people really checking up on me were other UC guys from my program. The agent who introduced me to the whole thing would call, or Dutch or Coop. From thousands of miles away, they would call me and check on me. No one else did.

Worse than all this, when I moved back home full time, I brought that Giovanni Gatto bastard with me. I can still see it in my mind, and it makes me sick—the things my kids had to see, the way I acted. I'd sit in front of the TV for hours on end, flipping through channels, with no idea what I was looking for. I'd have all my cell phones lined up on my coffee table in front of me, and I'd be waiting for one of them to ring. For *any* of them to ring.

I actually hoped that, say, Marco Barone would call me. He had sent me a text when the case went down, but then he went quiet. I think when he found out everybody had been arrested and I wasn't on the list, a lot of the guys like him must have panicked—guys like Gooms Bertelli, definitely. But here I was, so desperate for outside contact, for any kind of stimulation, I was waiting for a call from the criminals I'd been deceiving for two and a half years.

Of course, those phones never rang.

My wife would say, "Are you just going to sit there? Get up and do something."

"Leave me alone."

"Do something with the kids! Something! Anything!"

"Leave me alone. I can't go anywhere!"

Anna was infinitely more patient with me than I ever deserved. She recently described the situation in an interview with my coauthor:

> For him, it was like having a death in the family. The operation had become part of who he was. It was his reality more than we were his reality. To say the situation was trying would be an understatement. I don't know if he gives me much credit for it, but he was lucky to have me, because at least I understood what he was going through. A lot of spouses wouldn't. As happy as I was that it was over, I knew he had to go through a grieving process. Charlie Stango was a killer and a bad man, but my husband had grown very fond of him. Even though the whole point of the investigation was to make the arrests and put those people in jail, he was torn. It wasn't an easy thing for him to do. It wasn't easy for him to say, *Good, now it's over, and those people are in jail, because that's what I worked so hard to do all this time.* It was more like, *Do I really want to put Charlie in jail? I like the old bastard. I love him. I care about him.* For weeks, he just sat there on our couch, looking sick about what he'd done.

That's what made it so hard on both of us, and more so on the kids, who couldn't understand. The case was over, and their father was home. He hadn't been in their lives much during the investigation, but now that he was home, he still wasn't really there. It took a long time for him to come around and emotionally engage with us again, his real family, because he was grieving for that other family. And then having to go through what we went through with the government—basically abandoning us—and us trying to figure out how we were going to protect ourselves made things even worse. Even though my husband knew it was a bad situation for us and knew how close in proximity all those mob people were, he was still emotionally checked out. It was hard to get him to focus on the protection aspect of it when he was still caught up in grieving over what he had done to them.

What really grated on me was that he got to stay home and hide out, but the rest of us didn't. I still had to take the kids to school, still had to go out shopping, still had to be out there. There were a lot of things that had to be done, and we didn't get to stay home and hide in the house. He did.

Everything Anna said there is right, and every day I thank heaven that she stuck with me.

So, as I said, I was pretty much on lockdown. The only time I left our house was to sit in the backyard or, once in a while, go to the office. After the first group of the defendants had made bail, the best advice the bosses could offer me was "Lay low until we figure something out."

"Very helpful," I told them. "I'll be sure to deliver that message to my wife."

Finally, on one of my visits at the office, an experienced agent came up to me: "Hey, it's a good case. You did a great job. Congratulations. But do you really think you're going to be able to stay here?"

"What the hell are my options?" I asked. "What am I going to do? Quit? What am I going to do? This is my life!"

"Didn't anybody approach you yet? You know, for doing a risk assessment?"

"No."

The FBI agreed to do a risk assessment, and some guys came up from Washington. One agent did an assessment and submitted it to then-director James Comey, who reviewed it. In response, Comey dispatched a team led by his head of security. They came to our house a number of times, stayed in the area for three days, and finally sat down with Anna and me to go over the results in detail. The agent who had led the team had a little booklet with him, listing their findings. We were told that the formal report would be prepared later and copies would be provided to us, but their primary message was that the assessment's outcome was one of the worst.

"There's a serious threat here. We feel uncomfortable leaving you here in this house. That's how much of an issue this is. What we highly recommend is that you pack your bags—today."

Our initial reaction was "Well, we can't do that right now. We have kids in school. Work something out for us."

The team's findings drove home to me, in the starkest of terms, that for the safety and well-being of my family, I had absolutely no option but to retire from my department and enroll us in the relocation program. In the meantime, and until the paperwork for our move could be completed, an agent from the Newark division was appointed to head a local security team.

As it turned out, while the department heads in Washington argued over what program the funding for our relocation would come from, it took a full nine months to relocate us. I can't resist pointing out that in my previous law enforcement career, I had helped to place several informants and their families into witness protection—and not one of those cases had taken that long.

Although I was unable to work during those intervening months, my wife was still on the job as a serving police detective. And, yes, we had firearms in our house, and we both knew how to use them. But that was a worst-case solution. More important, we were obliged to spend long hours practicing evacuations with our kids. Think about it: explaining to preteen children that we needed to practice home evacuations in case men with guns came looking for their father.

Along with that, the kids had to be taught to use security measures. If something happened in the middle of the day and the children were in school, arrangements had to be made for their safety. The kids were trained to be suspicious of everyone.

Even simple things like riding their bicycles or playing outside with their friends were highly stressful for me and Anna. If a Lincoln Town Car or a Cadillac turned into our street, we would be on pins and needles. It usually turned out to be a car service dropping off a neighbor after work in Manhattan, but we could never be sure.

While the FBI had me laying low, waiting to be relocated, I received an unexpected request. I was provided the opportunity to travel to Europe to share my experiences with law enforcement and intelligence agencies. Careful arrangements were made to whisk me across the Atlantic.

After sharing my story with the attendees, we took a dinner break and a stroll outside the facility. One of the supervisors was busy filling out paperwork. He called out, asking what the date was. Someone responded, "September 28." It suddenly struck me that that was the same date I had been sworn in as a police officer twenty-six years earlier.

My career had officially come to an end—no retirement party, no awards ceremony, no official acknowledgment for my service, nothing. It was if I was never there.

My visit at the facility ended just before midnight, and I boarded a government-provided vessel to carry me across the English Channel. On boarding, I discovered that I was the only passenger on the boat. The captain jokingly told me that I could choose whatever seat was available. I chose instead to stand out on the bow and enjoy a view I would probably never again experience in my life.

Alone on the bow during the crossing, I called Anna and the kids to tell them where I was and to check on their security. I told Anna about my amazing experience and the synchronicity of this particular date.

I started to choke up as I explained to her that it was difficult for me to enjoy the experience because of the price my family had pay to for it. She could hear that I was becoming emotional and having trouble speaking. In the true fashion of this amazingly resilient woman, she explained to me that they were all safe back home and that I should just relax and enjoy the moment I was in. She told me how proud she was of what I had accomplished and how much I was loved by her and all four children.

After we ended our call, I spent a long, quiet moment just standing there, listening to the bow cutting through the water and gazing out at the flickering lights of the English coastline.

Despite all my worries and doubts, a solitary thought crystalized in my mind: *Not too bad for a neighborhood kid from Bayonne. Not too bad at all.*

———————

Our family did eventually relocate. Despite the change of environment, there remain too many unknowns for us to relax. The necessity for each of us to be vigilant continues to this day.

Making matters worse, each of us struggles with the fact that we had to leave behind everyone we knew and loved: our beloved relatives and friends, our longtime workmates, our children's treasured playmates. In a very real sense, we were forced to leave everything and everyone behind that *defined us*, both as individuals and as a family. It is a constant strain, but we are doing our best to build a new life.

As for my Giovanni ring, I removed it for the last time and returned it to the FBI, where it is stored in a locker, probably never to be seen again.